"These truthful, celebratory, inspiring and teachers of InsideOut have been creating sparks and lighting fires for young people in Detroit for two decades. The pieces, like the kids themselves, have grit, spirit, resilience, the breath of life."
—Edward Hirsch, president,
John Simon Guggenheim Memorial Foundation

"In her introduction to the anthology *To Light a Fire*, InsideOut Literary Arts Project founder Terry Blackhawk says, 'It's always an honor when students open up their lives for their teachers.' Blackhawk and her colleagues honor their readers by opening up their Detroit classrooms and telling their stories—stories of creating a safe space for creative expression by students, and stories of how those students inspired the authors' own poetry. The teaching methods vary, but the passion and compassion of the remarkable artists who have taught with InsideOut come through on every page of this collection, which illuminates a path for other writers who want to engage young people with the written word."
—Amy Swauger, director, Teachers & Writers Collaborative

"Educators nationwide are desperate for an antidote to student apathy and disengagement. InsideOut has the solution—give students compelling texts and invite them to respond to compelling tasks. The work described here goes beyond college and career readiness. These teachers are preparing students for life!"
—Carol Jago, longtime English teacher and past president
of the National Council of Teachers of English

"Terry Blackhawk's discovery of how art matters can't help but excite and inspire. Stories she shares of her experimental, ever-evolving InsideOut project remind us how and why a wrong-headed attitude toward the arts can sink a whole nation's boat. Through the poetry, storytelling, playwriting, and performances that she and other caring, recognized Detroit artists practice and profess, Blackhawk's high school and other institutional students broke past barriers that border the heart. In Jack London's enduring short story "To Build a Fire," the narrator says, 'He worked slowly and carefully, keenly aware of his danger.' *To Light a Fire* reignites that very same spark and flame. How much longer can we go on killing off, torturing, or warehousing our pitifully needed long-distance runners? Terry Blackhawk knows. This powerful anthology delivers."
—Al Young, former poet laureate of California

"Throughout *To Light a Fire,* adult and student writers reverberate as interchangeable mentors and mentees with emotional connections, heartfelt expressions, and emotional and provocative messages. Dr. Terry Blackhawk's vision for InsideOut and City Wide Poets, along with Peter Markus, writers-in-residence, teachers, and administrators, willingly nurture students' minds, hearts, and souls."

**—Toni S. Walters, PhD, professor emerita
of reading and language arts, Oakland University**

"*To Light a Fire* is an inspiration, a blessing, and a necessity. The various essays included serve as a guide, a success report, and a challenge to those who read it to initiate a project like InsideOut in schools throughout the country that have never offered their students the wonderful opportunity of transforming their experiences, imaginary and real, into literary art. This collection wisely begins with a chronology of events that led to the creation, development, and expansion of the InsideOut Literary Arts Project. But years before she founded this project in 1994, Dr. Terry Blackhawk was already incorporating some of its features by encouraging her students to write and perfect their poems. She also invited professional poets to her classes to share some of their own work and involve her students in discussions of what makes a poem a poem. I am happy for the publication of *To Light a Fire* and all the helpful information it contains. It is my hope that it will serve as an incentive to expand the program locally and nationally so that thousands of uninvolved students on all grade levels will discover how to bring to the surface the hidden poet in all of us."

**—Naomi Long Madgett, poet laureate for the City of Detroit
and author of *Pilgrim Journey***

"This luminous book speaks to the transformative power of poetry. Its brilliant, brave writing is poignant, generous, and deeply observant. Essays by talented InsideOut teachers with poems by their students will engage readers interested in literary arts, urban youth, learning communities, teaching and justice, and Detroit's vitality."

**—Susan Opotow, professor, John Jay College of Criminal Justice
and The Graduate Center, City University of New York**

# To *Light* a *Fire*

# To *Light* a *Fire*

## 20 Years with the InsideOut Literary Arts Project

EDITED BY Terry Blackhawk AND Peter Markus

WAYNE STATE UNIVERSITY PRESS
DETROIT

19 18 17 16 15                    5 4 3 2 1

ISBN 978-0-8143-4117-9 (paperback) / ISBN 978-0-8143-4118-6 (e-book)

Library of Congress Control Number: 2014959211

Publication of this book was made possible by a generous gift from The Meijer Foundation. Additional support provided by Michigan Council for Arts and Cultural Affairs and National Endowment for the Arts.

*Designed and typeset by Adam B. Bohannon*

*Composed in Chaparral*

# Contents

InsideOut Timeline      vii

Introduction: Patron Saint of the Soundless Gears      1
  *Terry Blackhawk*

How to Turn an Ordinary Floor into an Oceanside Beach
with One Hand: Field Notes Concerning the Precise
Location of the Imagination      30
  *Matthew Olzmann*

What Color Is in Between? Poetry and Creative Vision
in Children      36
  *Norene Cashen*

In the Dream      39
  *Robert Fanning*

Conduit: Connecting All the Stampeding Hearts      44
  *Jamaal May*

The Poet as Empathetic Witness      49
  *Suzanne Scarfone*

The Adolescent Heart      54
  *Julia Putnam*

Indelible Moments      59
  *John Rybicki*

What Poetry Has to Do with Any of It      66
  *Anna Clark*

Dangerous Acts      69
  *Nandi Comer*

Going Home      72
  *Gloria Nixon-John*

Sharing Voices, Acting Crazy      78
  *Cindy Frenkel*

Contents

Where the Word Is                                                    84
  Aricka Foreman

Mess Making                                                          88
  francine j. harris

To Love Something                                                    92
  Kristine Uyeda

Is a Change Gonna Come?                                              97
  Isaac Miller

However You May Say It                                               103
  Kristin Palm

Notes for that Screenplay One of Us Needs to Write                   107
  Stacy Parker Le Melle

I Named You the Honeycomb                                            113
  Alise Alousi

Langston's Hues                                                      117
  Chace Morris

A Nebulous Space                                                     120
  Anita Schmaltz

Split and Sprout from InsideOut                                      127
  Thomas Park

Conclusion: Inside My Magic Pencil                                   131
  Peter Markus

CONTRIBUTORS                                                         147

# InsideOut Timeline

**Summer 1994** Dr. Terry Blackhawk, English teacher at Mumford High School (1986–92) receives a letter from Mumford alumnus Robert Shaye inviting her to submit a proposal to the Four Friends Foundation to foster the literary arts among young people in Detroit.

**December 1994** InsideOut is founded with support from the Four Friends Foundation. Founding iO Board Members include Murray Jackson (1926–2002), Sterling C. Jones, Jr. (1927–2009), Deborah Thompson, Bill Harris, Gina Alexander Granger, Toni S. Walters, Janet McElrath, and Bob Shaye.

**January 13, 1995** InsideOut is incorporated. Programming begins at five Detroit Public Schools high schools: Cass Technical, Communication & Media Arts, Mumford, Henry Ford, and Davis Aerospace.

**May 1995** First annual iO year-end gala is held at the Serengeti Ballroom to unveil the first set of five InsideOut published literary magazines. iO year-end galas continue to be held across Detroit through 2009.

**1995–97** InsideOut conducts pilot programming in the five initial high schools during its first three years.

**September 1997** Terry Blackhawk founds Citywide Poets, an after-school poetry performance workshop geared toward high school writers who want to pursue writing more deeply. Citywide Poets makes its debut performance in the Detroit Renaissance Center before a national audience of educators at the National Council of Teachers of English Annual Convention.

**Fall 1997** InsideOut opens its first public office in the Palms Building on Woodward Avenue in downtown Detroit. Programming expands base to twelve schools.

**March 1998** Dr. Blackhawk attends organizational meeting of national writers-in-schools consortium, spearheaded by Writers in the Schools, Houston, Texas.

**Summer 1998** "Detroit Visions," a poetry and photography workshop focused on the city of Detroit, garners InsideOut its first funding from the Michigan Council for the Arts and Cultural Affairs. The Chrysler Corporation becomes iO's first corporate contributor.

**1999** InsideOut becomes a vendor with Detroit Public Schools, expanding into fifteen schools. iO receives the Michigan Community Arts Award from the Michigan Association of Community Arts Agencies.

**2000** InsideOut grows to serve students in twenty-one schools, including elementary and middle schools. Dr. Terry Blackhawk receives the Michigan Governor's Award for Arts Education. First iO collaboration with Detroit PuppetART Theater, Detroit Open School.

**2001** Naomi Long Madgett, Detroit Poet Laureate, initiates Lotus Press High School Poetry Prize to be awarded annually to an iO student.

**2001** iO launches the "Central Playwriting Project," which sent renowned playwright Ron Milner (1938–2004) to work with students at Central High School and its feeder school, Longfellow Middle. A culminating performance in 2002, "Keeping It Real: Making It Art," brought Milner's iO students to Wayne State's Studio Theatre for a public performance.

**2001–4** iO partners with PEN Faulkner Visiting Authors Program to bring touring fiction writers into high schools to discuss their latest books.

**Spring 2002** iO launches first dual elementary school collaboration with PuppetART featuring residencies combining storytelling and puppetry, with joint premiers at PuppetART's downtown theater: Stewart and Glazer (2002, 2004, 2005), Detroit Open and Glazer (2005), Bennett and Burns (2008).

**September 2002** Unexpected loss of one-third of iO's funding.

**March 2003** InsideOut's first fundraising event is held at Marygrove College.

**Fall 2003** InsideOut signs its first multi-year contract with Detroit Public Schools.

**2004** InsideOut expands to twenty-three schools. iO receives a three-year grant of $100,000 per year from the Skillman Foundation's Youth Arts Community Development initiative to support its after school work with Citywide Poets.

**May 2005** InsideOut's 10th Anniversary Fundraiser at Detroit's Historic Gem Theater featuring Nikki Giovanni as guest speaker.

**Fall 2005** InsideOut enters a partnership with the University of Michigan's MFA Program (now Helen Zell Writers' Program), which awards four MFA students "Civitas" fellowships to serve as InsideOut writers-in-residence. iO implements the first of its annual evaluations, which have steadily shown significant impact on students' writing skills, college readiness, confidence, self-esteem, and positive attitude toward reading and writing.

**Fall 2007** InsideOut receives Humanities Award from Wayne County Commission for Arts, History and Humanities. iO institutes pilot Voices Program at the high school level to reach more students through writing across curriculum programs, writing centers, and increased writers' service.

**May 2008** InsideOut collaborates with the Detroit Opera House; third and fourth graders from DPS's Hanstein Elementary School write and perform "The Ringer of the Moon," an original opera.

**Fall 2009** InsideOut offers programming to students in thirty schools including schools in Highland Park and South Lake. In a ceremony held at the White House, InsideOut receives the National Arts and Humanities Youth Program Award (then "Coming Up Taller") from the President's Committee on the Arts and the Humanities presented by Michelle Obama.

**Fall 2010** InsideOut receives $100,000 Erb Family Foundation grant for "Women Influence Words," community-wide programming focused on women writers, in conjunction with a Big Read grant allowing iO to bring the work of Emily Dickinson to Detroit students and families.

**October 2010** In a gala at the Gem Theater, iO presents Detroit Poet Laureate Naomi Long Madgett with the first iO Literary Legacy Award.

**January 2011** InsideOut moves its offices to Wayne State University.

**March 2011** InsideOut receives $80,000 Learning in the Arts grant, the second largest in the nation, from the National Endowment for the Arts to expand its Voices Program.

**April 2011** First annual high school writers' conference *Who Understands Me But Me?* brings together Detroit Public Schools students from iO high schools for a day of workshops and readings.

**May 2011** A delegation of iO youth is invited to the White House to participate in a poetry workshop.

**July 2011** InsideOut's Slam Team takes fourth place at Brave New Voices International Youth Poetry Slam Festival before an audience of over 3,000 at the San Francisco Opera House.

**November 2011** InsideOut is the only Detroit youth agency to receive the $50,000 Sun Life Rising Star Award two years in a row.

**2012** InsideOut receives the Champions in Action Award from Charter One. New Detroit recognizes iO with its Closing the Gap Award.

**2011–13** End-of-year *Get Versed* showcases at Detroit Institute of Arts Film Theatre feature iO students from grades three through twelve in multi-genre poetry performances of music, art, dance, and video.

**October 2013** iO is featured on the PBS NewsHour series "Where Poetry Lives," created by US Poet Laureate Natasha Trethewey. iO expands to Oakland County by launching service to schools in Oak Park and Pontiac.

**2014** iO board adopts new "eye-opening" logo to reflect nickname and enhanced brand—"iO."

**April 2015** Terry Blackhawk announces her retirement. A nationwide search for a new director begins.

# Introduction: Patron Saint of the Soundless Gears

*Terry Blackhawk*


Twenty years. It's a marvel to me that InsideOut Literary Arts Project, with its roots in my teaching so many years ago, should have grown into the organization that it is today. From humble beginnings in a handful of Detroit classrooms, we have become one of the premier writers-in-schools programs in the nation, with service to some 5,000 K–12 students per year and the publication of over 400 separate school literary journals since our inception. We have built a reputation for caring, excellence, and innovation, and have earned the support of loyal followers and the gratitude of students, alumni, parents, teachers, and principals. We have been awarded by the White House and featured on the PBS NewsHour, and our youth have been recognized for their creativity and performances on stages from the Kennedy Center to the San Francisco Opera House. The story of our history as a nonprofit would require a book unto itself, but since the organization grew from the practices I discovered in my creative writing classrooms in Detroit, first at Mumford High School and then at Communication and Media Arts High School, I will start at the very beginning.

My years as an English teacher at Mumford initiated one of the most creative and experimental periods of my teaching career. I was fortunate to find myself in a comprehensive high school, full of interesting, urban teens, well before standardized testing and odious practices such as "zero tolerance" achieved such dominance. I was also fortunate to work in a school with colleagues who themselves engaged in the arts and where classes in the visual arts, vocal and instrumental music, drama, and radio/TV/speech weren't taken for granted. In spring 1987, English department chair Elaine Green challenged us teachers to submit poems for a brand-new school literary publication to feature work by staff and students. Writing my first poem in over twenty years for Mumford's *Style!*—an intensely moving experience that someone later identified for me as a "muse attack"—set me on my path as a poet. Shortly thereafter, in addition to regular English classes, I had the good fortune of teaching several sections of "Writing Improvement"—an elective that, while usually taught as a remedial course, was open-ended and enabled me to try new teaching methods. I was interested in Writing Process Pedagogy, which was relatively new at the time, and I incorporated my classroom work teaching writing into my PhD studies in Reading and Language Arts education at Oakland University.

I never set out to be an activist, but the excitement of inciting writing—for myself and for my students—just took hold. Within a year, I had reached out to the poetry world in order to develop and grow as a poet. Taking seminars, journeying to the Frost Place, and joining a poetry group with Gloria Nixon-John were early milestones. I gained inspiration from Louise Harrison, who led the Michigan Youth Arts Festival's Creative Writing Awards, and shared much with poet and fellow teacher Dawn McDuffie. And I reached out to bring the world of writing into our school. Michigan's now-defunct Creative Writers in Schools program offered a roster of writers to choose from and grants for short residencies in the spring. The Detroit Council for the Arts also offered grants, and I found other funding that enabled me to bring in playwrights, fiction writers, storytellers, and poets to work with our students.

And oh, the Mumford students! I'm sure the light of memory casts a rosy glow as I look back, but so many eager, creative beings passed through my classroom doors. Every now and then I'll hear from some of those students. Once at Detroit Metro Airport, I bumped into Meta who told me, with a kind of conspiratorial smile, that she had become a Language Arts teacher. Some students look me up on Facebook. Jervante reminded me recently of an assignment in which I had asked students to write poems of praise to one another. Our creative writing classes were small communities where, as one student wrote at the end of the year when I had them put comments and reflections about the class on large sheets of paper, "We were neither black nor white in here, just gray." I'm not sure how to interpret this. "Gray" isn't particularly inspiring and using poetry written from the African American experience was always a cornerstone of my teaching, with poets like Lucille Clifton and Yusef Komunyakaa helping pave the way for students' own brave writing. I don't believe this student felt that her identity was obliterated. There were no white students in the class. Rather, I like to think she was acknowledging the comfort she felt with a white teacher who attempted, as best she could, to honor everyone's stories.

One powerful memory of those stories comes from Bill Harris's residency at Mumford. Bill was one of the first writers I reached out to through the Michigan Council for the Arts Creative Writers in Schools program. When I discovered his name in the council's statewide roster provided for teachers, I eagerly contacted him, thinking that he would make a good role model for my male students in particular. Newly returned to Detroit from New York City where he had written plays for the New Federal Theatre and worked as a producer for Harlem's Jazzmobile, Bill was to become a Detroit literary legend. It was easy to see why, even then. The students loved his weekly visits and what I can only describe as his "bracing" presence in the classroom—a mixture of humor, candor, challenge, respect, and utmost cool. One day, Angela burst into Room 201 to announce to me, "Mrs. Blackhawk, I've written a play!" Although there had been no "assignment," Bill's influence as a playwright had clearly borne fruit.

For her play, "Hard to Serve," Angela created parts with specific members of the class in mind, cast for their personalities although not for their life experiences. Her mother was an instructor for a social services agency and worked with youth in a class that was labeled "hard to serve"—a label that Angela saw as deeply disrespectful, and one that, for me, echoes right up there with *underprivileged, disadvantaged, at risk, disengaged*, and all the other all-too-common labels that identify students as defective and lacking. Angela adopted a readers' theatre structure for the play in which each of her classmates took the part of an adjudicated youth assigned to a "hard to serve" classroom. Each character's life had been marked by a particular urban ill—child abuse, homelessness, gangs, drugs—but they supported one another, and the dialogue was moving and honest as they confronted a new student assigned to the class who felt socially superior and certain that he "didn't belong" with them. The play resolves as the outsider comes to recognize his arrogance and accept the humanity of his peers.

With Bill's guidance, we rehearsed Angela's play and took it on the road, playing at the United Black Artists (UBA) annual festival as well as Wayne County Community College and Mumford. The play was included along with many noted African American authors in the UBA anthology *Roots and Blossoms*, and Angela won a drama award in the Michigan Youth Arts Festival, receiving acceptance at Western Michigan University largely on the basis of her creative writing. Working with Angela's play was one of my first experiences of taking youth voices out into the world beyond the classroom. It was exciting to guide a project that was completely initiated by students. Their energy and camaraderie were infectious, and with extra hours in rehearsals and treks to sites in the community outside of the school, we really began to feel like family.

It was that same year, 1989, when a chance encounter at the copy machine in the Mumford library would set my life in a completely different direction. Bob Shaye, a noted Mumford alumnus and founder of New Line Cinema, was in town, recruiting his alma mater's marching band for *The Book of Love*, a movie he was directing. Principal Robin Oden introduced us and shortly thereafter I wrote to Mr. Shaye to ask for support in the publication of *Style!* He kindly responded with funding that covered the first professional printing of the magazine. With his support and funding from the various grants I was able to cobble together, many writers came to our classrooms, and Mumford became the site of the most thriving high school literary scene in the city.

Guest poets and writers such as Bill Harris invigorated my classroom in ways I could not have thought possible. Each writer stirred up a new mix. I looked forward to their visits as much as my students, and I count myself fortunate to have worked with and learned from so many amazing individuals. It kind of reads like a who's who of the Detroit area and/or visiting writers who came to my classes in those pre-iO years: Toi Derricotte, Naomi Long Madgett, Eugene Redmond, Leslie Reese, Nubia Kai, Selene de Madeiros, Kofi Natambu, Anne Finger, Brenda Flanagan, Kaleema

Hasan, Joe Matuzak, Josie Kearns, Therese Becker, Larry Pike, and Quincy Troupe. Even John Sinclair (Meta's uncle) joined us, and of course Bill Harris, who was an amazing force with the students at Mumford for several years.

Some writers came for repeated visits, but Toi Derricotte's single visit to my class stands out all on its own. I met Toi at the Frost Place in 1988. She was their festival's guest poet, and the fact that she was a Detroiter by birth gave us much to talk about. When she next came to Detroit to see her mother, we discussed a possible visit to my classroom, and we were able to put it together the following spring. Her visit was transformative. When Toi, with her warmth and humor and grace, shared poems about the abuse she suffered at the hands of her father, it seemed the floodgates opened for my students as they began to write. There was a new atmosphere in the room, a concentration and an intensity all its own, and when the students shared what they had written, I saw sides of them that I had never seen before. The experience made me want to be more like Toi, generous and open in my teaching, and showed me how writing could be a healing force in students' lives.

It's always an honor when students open up their lives for their teachers, and I found that teaching creative writing helped me to know my students more closely than ever before. Here's Nashawn Reed, using an assignment on the myth of Orpheus, to write about her late father and other loved ones.

**Orpheus Variations**
*i. Father*
Upon white satin and lace
he lies motionless.
His black wavy hair and
thin moustache complement
the pale, cold skin.
Pinstripes travel vertically
down the navy blue suit
like roads on a map
leading nowhere now.

A glint of a thin, gold pin
accents the lapel.
A cherry red rose
where the heart once lived.


*ii. Ghost*
A cool breeze flows through
what used to be your bedroom,
as I sleep with my face
compressed into the pillow.
Three white, hooded images
approach my bedside.
I know it's you.
A masculine hand grasps
the crown of my head,
keeping me still.
The hand is yours.
Your voice whispers to me
that everything's okay
but angels hum like a church
choir and my scream for help
is mute, as suddenly,
you disappear.


*iii. Juanita*
I step through a mirror
extending a hand to you.
I'm here as your savior
to rescue you from
the unliving.
You mustn't stay long
or death will love
you too much.
Let our joyous emotions
guide us. Let
shattered shards of mirrored glass
mark our presence

and reflect our descent down
the white spiral staircase.
Welcome home, Juanita.

An assignment to write from a childhood memory prompted Nicole May's "My First Day in Second Grade," which begins with the taunts she suffered growing up as a biracial child.

I remember my tan skin
burning with humiliation
as little white girls
shook their blond-
capped heads, saying
furiously, "You can't
be everything!"

And I remember the heels
of my feet moving up and
down to tilt the rockers
of the reading chair
in hope of fading out
the voices of the little black
girls that said with conviction,
"One drop and you're black!"

I squeeze my eyes shut.
My knuckles turn white
and my thoughts scream:
But what about the rest
of the world that runs
through my veins? Each atom
collides with another to
form what is not only
African,
Caucasian,
Native American,
or Hispanic—

but a new world that no
kind but my own can comprehend.

I'm glad that my students felt safe enough to reach into personal material, and I like to think that the imaginative writing skills that I stressed gave them tools of mastery. These were not first drafts, but writings that consciously attempted to use the craft of poetry—precise word choice, concrete nouns, metaphor, sensory imagery, active verbs, voice, musicality of language—bearing in mind that, to paraphrase Grace Paley, "one goes to the school of poetry in order to write prose." Some of their images have stayed with me, indelibly. A ninth grader—who wrote for the first time about a drive-by shooting she narrowly escaped when she was twelve—described coming into her living room to find her "fish gasping on the floor" and a shattered aquarium before opening the door to carnage on her front porch. A junior, who used metaphors of war to describe sexual abuse she endured at age nine, ended her poem with surrender to her abuser as she lay down on the bed to "once again/become a woman." She wrote this poem in the fall and shared it, with a kind of forced bravado, for a stunned and silent class. The following spring, when I was asking students to comment on what the year had meant to them, one boy complimented her courage in sharing the poem in November. His affirmation of her remains one of my proudest teaching moments.

From 1989 to 2001, the Detroit Institute of Arts sponsored the Student Writing about Art project that each year sent slides of ten treasures from the museum to teachers in Detroit Public Schools classrooms across the city, and each year I launched my Creative Writing classes immersed in this richness. After viewing, discussing, and writing about everything art—from Van Gogh to Frankenthaler to ancient Egyptian amulets and African sculpture—students visited the DIA to see the works up close in the galleries, and some even saw their writings printed alongside the images in the project's culminating publication. I was proud that phrases from my students' work were selected as titles of these beautiful anthologies more than once. *Blues Remedy, Thunderous Words, Where Stories Are Told, My Poetry Is Music*—the artworks, the poems, and the voices of students themselves still live in my mind. One favorite came from a thoughtful Mumford senior, a quiet student, whose response to the abstract, amorphous pour of Helen Frankenthaler's "The Bay" prompted this philosophical poem.

### The Bay

*(after Helen Frankenthaler)*

The paint splatters everywhere
a blue river
representing our thoughts
going in all directions
reaching out
hoping to be heard.
In our subconscious
we see a million colors
yet our conventional mind
suppresses them.
As humans, we are abstract
creatures. We don't
fit in, but when we are absorbed
into nature
as the green absorbs
the blue, we blend
with all that is in
the universe.

GARY WILLIAMS

Abstraction also inspired ninth grader Michael McElrath, who gave Alvin Loving's "J. E. and the Uptown A's"—a three-dimensional collage of torn paper and cardboard cut-outs, intersecting spirals, planes, and squares—a distinctly Detroit habitation.

### Thunderous Words

Anger is the graffiti of your
mind.
The monster of content.
A black whole of chaos

Powerful and strong
The high energy of the world
Stabs of sharp envy—
Oh how graphic its rampage
Its diverse language of thunderous
words
A boisterous disorder
I'd love to leave
In a city where hearts
are like sharp rocks.

Writing about, or through, visual art has a marvelous way of taking a writer outside of herself and into that state called "flow" where attention to the immediate world seems to drop away. I believe that, in the words of my poetry mentor Stephen Dunn, it's important to get out of our "conventional, work-a-day mind and . . . say something that we do not know we are capable of saying." I suspect that such "flow" existed for Gary, as he discovered that we "are abstract creatures" *during* the process of writing and not, as Gertrude Stein would say, "ahead of time. In a thought." Absorption in art, meditating, and most of all free writing all allow for this. I started many writing classes free writing along with my students, enjoying experiencing the pen as a direct conduit to the brain. "Don't think," I was fond of telling my students. "Write!" Another mantra, often displayed in my room, was E. M. Forster's "How do I know what I think until I see what I say?" This approach encourages students to trust their associative, unconscious minds. allowing meanings to come in obliquely, as if from the corner of the eye.

Words themselves, the "stuff" of language, can trigger ideas. An assignment to weave the arbitrary phrase "the sleep of this night deepens" into a poem along with other designated words such as "flagpole" and "whistle" led to this eerie poem.

### Dusk
Noon was prolonged and evening now deepens.
The wind whistles me to the window.

The leaves race in a marathon for charity
While the flag dances frantically on its thin, tin leg.
MURRAY RADNEY

A Moebius strip exercise from *The Adventures of Dr. Alphabet*, in which students write non-stop, pulling the mysteriously one-sided yet two-sided Moebius beneath their pens, is fascinating enough on its own. Combined with contemplation of a surrealistic photograph, it inspired eleventh grader Nandi Comer's lovely poem.

**Three Moons**

When you bring me my three moons
and let the hills turn wild blue
the sand will sparkle
like stars

If the stars turn wild with envy
from no brighter shine
change them into sapphire
and my sky, make it burgundy
to match sunset waters

Lift me to sit under
fuchsia trees and wait for
my winds to
bring me my three moons.

The interplay between my mind and the students'—the way they picked up the ball and ran with ideas and assignments—made my early years as a teacher of creative writing very rich indeed. But I would never have assigned this topic, which won First Prize for Poetry in the *Detroit Free Press* 1991 High School Student Writing Awards for its author.

**For Mrs. Blackhawk**
We were unsuspecting
when we arrived.

Our pains were separate.
We each built a dam of reservation
and fear.
But, like a quiet tornado, you
twisted with energy—
swooping everything
into your arms, pulling
down our fortresses.
Our emotions exploded like
geysers and at first some of us
were ashamed. We felt alien
to each other—not because we
didn't endure pain, but because
we hadn't expressed ourselves
before. Our rivers carried
the same current, but they seemed
so different, one from another.
Unselfishly, you became the strait
through which we passed.
We then found a common place
where we could seek solace
in others' hearts.

NICOLE MAY

This poem still humbles me. A teacher could not ask for more.

Ever restless and eager to pursue poetry in a deeper manner, I applied for a sabbatical from the National Endowment for the Humanities in 1992–93 to study the life and work of Emily Dickinson. The sabbatical year brought writing, travel, scholarship and an invaluable feeling of renewal. After a year away and still imprinted by the hills of northern California where I had squeezed in a last-minute storytelling workshop with Laura Simms, I prepared to meet my 175 students: five ninth grade Writing Improvement classes at Communication and Media Arts High School. Igniting creativity and inciting writing were, as before, my personal mission. Although CMA was not his alma mater, I reached out to Bob Shaye again in early 1994 and again he kindly offered his support.

The resulting journal, *Passages II*, featuring the work of my CMA students, was a lively and touching portrait of Detroit teens through their poetry, stories and visual art. I sent copies to Bob with thank-you notes from the students, and in the summer of 1994 I received a letter suggesting that I write a proposal to his family foundation. Expanding the literary activism I enjoyed with my high school students, he suggested, would be "a supremely valuable cultural goal," and he proposed that with his help I form an organization to take us "citywide." I often describe myself as the fairy godmother of iO largely because of this encounter. And there was something magical about it. You're on a journey through a deep forest (or at a copy machine in a school library) when you meet a magical being. The being grants three wishes, or poses three questions or, in my case, makes a suggestion, and you are suddenly on a different path.

So, in fall 1994, I gathered a group of friends, educators, and writers and together we formed a board of directors, drafted bylaws, applied for nonprofit status, and set things underway. Our first task was to decide on a name, so we drew up a ballot and presented it to students in pilot classrooms in five high schools. InsideOut was the clear choice. I wish I had a copy of that ballot, but I can still see Martinique, a tenth grader, raising her hand after my class had voted to say, "This means we are bringing what is inside of us out into the world through our writing." These words still resonate in iO's mission today.

Duly named, iO began in five Detroit high schools. A couple of years later we added a middle school, an elementary school, and finally grew into Detroit's largest literary nonprofit, a writers-in-residence program that serves thousands of students each year in K–12 schools across our city. The mission of iO is to encourage young writers to "think broadly, create bravely, and share their voices with the wider world," and although we have added many components and variations on these themes, the three pillars of iO have not changed since the first day: weekly classroom visits by a writer-in-residence, the publication of a literary journal for each school, and myriad ways of bringing writing into the community.

Tens of thousands of stories could be told about the writers and students and the poems that have been created over the years at iO. Our goal for this anthology is to give a taste of some of them through the eyes of veteran iO writers. One of my favorite memories from iO's first official year is when Alvin Aubert, a beloved friend who passed away in January 2014, came to my class at CMA. A major poet, scholar, editor, retired English professor, and founder of *Obsidian: Black Literature in Review*, Alvin had a great wit, a wonderful laugh, and he was full of stories—stories of his French, Cajun, Native American, African ancestry and upbringing in a Mississippi River town on the periphery of Cajun country. Alvin Aubert's was a kind but imposing presence, and he brought real gravitas to my students. He inspired them with his openness to feeling, tearing up once as he shared a poem about the loss of a child by his friend Gerald Barrax, and presenting a compassionate role model to young men in particular. He was exacting, encouraging students to think carefully and to weigh the necessity of every single word. This poem, inspired by Yusef Komunyaaka's "Venus's Flytraps," which I often use as a prompt for writing about childhood, was begun in an earlier class and then crafted under Alvin's guidance.

### Ice Kingdom
Wearing Moonboots two sizes too big
I hike across a field of snow.
I dodge ice bullets
Thrown by my older brothers
To reach my hideaway
Where ice crystals hang from
A leafless tree.
The ground looks like frozen sky
And a mile-long field
Stretches behind me.
I know Mama said not to play
On the ice on the pond
Behind the train tracks—

And don't get your hair wet
And don't talk back

And don't wear your good shoes outside.

Mama said a lot of stuff.

But as I step on the ice
With the largest icicle
As my wand
I am the ice princess, Quiana
Ruler of the pond behind the tracks.

QUIANA WILLIAMS

Her line "Mama said a lot of stuff" especially appealed to Alvin, and I can still hear the affirmation in his voice as he read it aloud to the class, and then repeated it slowly, as if feeling its weight. Yep. Mama said a lot of stuff. It still rings true.

When Peter Markus and I were talking over a possible title for this collection, my first thought was "To Light a Fire," which springs from a motto adopted from the great Irish poet William Butler Yeats that "education is not the filling of a pail, but the lighting of a fire." I first heard that phrase in 1998 when I made the first of many visits to Houston's Writers in the Schools (WITS) headquarters, and it became a kind of mantra for me. A serendipitous contact I made at a literary table during a visit to Seattle's 1997 Bumbershoot Festival led me to WITS, to finding my "tribe" and ultimately joining the first of many gatherings that brought together fellow writers-in-schools leaders from across the country. Who knew there were other people around the country doing this work—savvy, inventive folk who believed that lighting fires, not filling pails, was the best way to help children learn.

"Filling" puts me in mind of the cartoon of the student's head as an empty vessel, with the lid (i.e., the cranium) turned sideways, and a faucet of knowledge pouring in from above—quite the opposite of getting students engaged and giving them the tools, the inspiration, and the creative fire to tell the world who they are. As iO has grown, we have taken our place alongside many nonprofits that intervene for the better in the lives of Detroit students, but I like to think that this fire, this essential gift of self-expression, sets us apart. iO is not a tutoring program, although one-on-one adult-youth relationships are essential to our work. We do not focus on test scores, although teacher after teacher will tell of academic improvement and greater classroom engagement thanks to iO. One "best practice" (although I'm getting kind of sick of that jargon) in the field of youth arts development is that young people work with "skilled practitioners" of the arts, so we pay iO's fabulous teaching artists a decent wage. And, as one Detroit leader said to me recently, iO is not "a parachute drop." We do not come and go as an organization. Pete also suggested "A Beautiful House," from a favorite quote of his from the mystic poet Hafiz: "Our words become the house we live in." I like that for its stability. We have been in Detroit schools and classrooms for a long time, building rich relationships, serving thousands of students per year, and building a beautiful house along the way.

Much is written of late about the need for creativity in education. The Arts Council of England, a country that actually invests in creative writing, puts it this way:

> In both education and arts policies in the last few years, there has been an emphasis on creativity as a vital skill and on the significance of cultural experiences for young people. The central tenets of creativity—supporting imaginative activity based on exploring alternatives, taking risks, developing original ideas, and solving problems—fit well with what writers in schools offer. Writers in schools can help to show how the basic skill of writing can be linked to creative thinking. This emphasis on creativity leads teachers to consider the implications for their classrooms. They need to experiment and try things out for themselves and develop pedagogies that encourage the same qualities in their pupils. If creativity is to flourish, then a different set of classroom pedagogies is needed. One teacher observed, "It is a change of mindset and how you want learning to take place in the classroom. It is teaching in a creative way that is crucial."

I am fortunate that poetry found me when it did and that as a result I started to develop, or rediscover, the creative mindset mentioned above. Just as the writers who came into my classrooms modeled creative pedagogy for me, the writers you will meet here come to the classroom not as authority figures, but as guides and coaches. They show the many ways the iO magic (i.e., creative writing and creative thinking) happens throughout the course of their weekly visits into Detroit's K–12 classrooms. They describe love of language, excursions into imagination, hearts that refuse to break no matter what; how a writer who listens, mentors, and believes can help a student find her voice; the despair that comes when children can be so lost, regardless; the way poems themselves can light fires; and the connections that are forged with teachers. They also describe the difficulties of getting through to kids, the challenges of oversized classrooms, and the angst and personal uncertainties about doing the right thing. The essays will move you and, perhaps best of all, you will get to know the beautiful spirits of the children of Detroit.

One such beautiful spirit was Shysuaune (pronounced Shy-Juan) Taylor, who I had the privilege of teaching in grades nine through eleven, my last three years of public school teaching. He was a gifted writer and clearly a student who wanted to make a difference in the world. He was part of a group of students that were a creative writing teacher's dream team—students who worked hard and loved writing and made a point of taking care of others as well as one another. One year, for instance, he and his peers organized an Easter basket drive for homeless children all by themselves. Shysuaune sought out personal opportunities as well, spending a month in ninth grade at the High Scope youth leadership camp and pursuing and performing his writing in venues around Detroit. He took statewide and local prizes for his writing and was one of the editors of CMA's literary magazine, *Soliloquy*. I'm especially proud that he encouraged one of his best friends to transfer to our school in order to "work with" me.

Over the three years that he was my student, I saw Shysuaune grow more serious and take more risks with his writing, but it wasn't until later that I learned his grandmother was a drug dealer. She figures in his poems each year, and it's interesting to watch the way his portrayals of her evolve. In grade nine she has a smile like a "warm summer sun," and she is sweet "as gingerbread," and predictably sentimental. In grade ten, a poem about her drug house, although not overtly identified as such, features a gun pressed against his temple, and the repeated refrain of police car lights "red blue / red blue // red blue / red blue." By eleventh grade, in 1996, her personality becomes clearer, somewhat satirized and a bit edgy. In "Grandma Speaks Musik" the first line is "Grandma takes a toke . . ." After high school, when he was nineteen, Shysuaune finally confronted the devastation caused by his grandmother's life of crime.

**Black Boy Blues**
baby black boy
learns his a, b, c's
baby black boy
learns his a, b, c's
A.B.C.R.A.C.K. recipes
Boiling water, baking soda
Burning broken wire hangers.

mama don't know granny is into plague retail
mama don't know granny is into plague retail
Watch baby black hands trace
deadly outlines of overdosed
souls quivering on the floor

Baby black boy eyes watch
dream smoke rise
from glass
pipes

Baby black boy eyes watch
dream smoke rise
from glass
pipes

Burning away bills, food, hungry baby mouths
baby boy black learns his 1, 2, 3's
baby boy black learns his 1, 2, 3's

1, 2, 3 ounces of Cocaine
to be made into
     rock
         crystallized
           worlds

baby boy black learns his 1, 2, 3's
baby boy black learns his 1, 2, 3's
1, 2, 3 ounces of Cocaine
to be made into
     rock
         crystallized
           worlds

sing the song of make believe baby boy black
sing the song of make believe baby boy black
as you watch the gun
being put to granny's head
and she
clicks
and she
clicks
and she
clicks

make believe
you are unaware
make believe
you are not scared
make believe
you don't know the recipe
for
     horror

This poem was featured in *You Hear Me? Poems and Writings by Teen-age Boys* published by Candlewick Press in 2000. Author, poet, and editor Betsy Franco got wind of iO through an article in *People* just as she was pitching the idea of the anthology to Candlewick. She solicited from me poems by young Detroit men, to support her proposal, and ultimately included over twenty of those poems in this award-winning anthology, which has gone into numerous printings. Shysuaune served as her editorial consultant, and she could not say enough about his participation, thoughtfulness, and wisdom. He was one of the first alumni who we trusted to serve as an iO poet-in-residence himself, earning rave reviews, even as a young teaching artist, first with sixth graders and later with youth at an alternative high school. The title he gave to Crosman High School's literary journal, *Above, Not Beneath*, capsulizes iO's understandings about the potential and struggles of Detroit's young people. Shysuaune died suddenly in 2002, but I'm ever grateful that iO helped him develop and share his talent. Shysuaune loved poetry. He lives in my mind as a youth who was unafraid, the epitome of why iO carries on. Our city needs nothing less than young people who are unafraid to tell the world who they are.

iO's mission directs us "to share students' voices with the wider world," and we fulfill this through extensive publications and performances. And so each iO school receives its own year-end literary publication—with titles like *The Hues of Langston, The Color of Our Voices, Ink on the Tracks, The Purple Door, Jambo, The Other World*, and many, many more. Over 400 such titles in the past 20 years have been published, and each year we organize a year-end, in-school gala celebrating the literary journals with each school's students, staff, and parents. One of the biggest payoffs of the year for me is the light in children's eyes when they see the books, *their books*, for the first time, with their names in them, and pore over them, sharing them with friends, and signing in true authorial fashion for one another. Through in-school publications, through Citywide Poets—iO's after-school spoken word and poetry slam program—through social media and dozens of public performances each year, iO gives young people the "author-ity" of being authors, thus helping Mr. Shaye to realize that valuable cultural goal.

But underlying these successes is our bedrock: iO changes and often saves lives. iO alumna Shirley Bolden, mentioned in Gloria Nixon-John's essay, will tell you flat out—that is her story. These days I find her on Facebook, celebrating the teaching she is doing, determined in her mission to bring the power of voice and self-confidence to more young people—to pass on the gift of iO. A post in June 2014 featured a nice year-end surprise: her students had left a dozen red roses arranged across the windshield of her car.

In June 2014, I was in on another teacher's surprise. I had been invited to Harms Elementary School on Detroit's southwest side to assist in a celebration of young authors sponsored by a lovely philanthropic group, Executive Women Incorporated, who had adopted the school. After I tore the wrapper off the poster-sized reproduction of the cover of the first prizewinner, "The Fire-breathing Strawberry," the EWI team had an announcement to make. It seems that they recently met with the teachers at Harms to ask how they could help the school next year. Would the teachers like more computers? Field trips? One teacher, Mr. Eric, asked for iO. He'd worked in two schools with our program, and his persuasiveness won the day. When the director of EWI announced that iO would be in their school next year, Mr. Eric was in tears. We were actually all a bit weepy, to tell the truth, and I received one of the best hugs ever from that big-hearted man who could barely contain his emotion and his joy. Two kids, he said. We'd reached a lot of kids, but we'd saved two. Classroom teachers with iO writers form terrific partnerships, nurturing creativity by teachers as well. In fact, Mr. Eric is not the first Detroit teacher who has lobbied, cajoled, or organized to keep "their" iO writer in place. The essays in this book show how delicate and strong those relationships can be.

Each of the contributors to this volume has touched hundreds, if not thousands, of students, and each has touched me in more ways than I can say. Gloria Nixon-John, mentioned above. Peter Markus, who has been with iO since Day One and is the rock upon which our foundation is built. Words fail me when I try to describe my good brother Pete, but readers can see him in action at www.insideout-detroit.org or the PBS NewsHour, which profiled iO as part of US Poet Laureate Natasha Trethewey's series "Where Poetry Lives" in October 2013. Another rock is Alise Alousi, a gifted poet and iO's indispensable Associate Director whose overall program management and leadership on projects such as our annual high school writing conference, college essay writing workshops, and more oil the gears and keep the complicated iO machine running smoothly.

I am grateful for writers who have moved away—Thomas Park, Kristin Palm, francine j. harris, Stacy Parker LeMelle—and who (although I miss them!) happily carried on this work with other organizations in California, Michigan, and Texas, or, in Thomas's case, created an iO-inspired literary arts program from scratch in North Carolina. And I am grateful for those who stay, reinventing, refining their skills and stepping up to pitch in. I am thinking here of Norene Cashen, who has taught at all grade levels, who coordinates Citywide Poets, and whose students from Bennett Elementary have written and performed original songs for our year-end citywide gala celebration, *Get Versed,* at the Detroit Institute of Arts; and of Anna Clark, who brings her talents as a journalist, blogger, and editor of the fabulous *A Detroit Anthology*, who pitched in on a Shakespeare video project in addition to her regular residency with students at Detroit School of Arts. I am grateful for Kristine Uyeda, point person for iO's yearlong "Big Read" that brought a host of Emily Dickinson events to Detroit in 2011. Kristine also helped to craft and implement a poetry-based middle school Social Studies curriculum that brought the blues, Robert Hayden, the Underground Railroad, and the Diego Rivera murals to bear on the students' understanding of Detroit's African American legacy and history of industrialization.

Some iO writers bring passion fueled by the fires of personal and transformative experiences that help young writers to open and feel safe in sharing their life stories. John Rybicki, whose students' poems were read in New York City at the tenth-anniversary commemoration of the destruction of the World Trade Center, and Cindy Frenkel come to mind here. Others have brought a flair for the dramatic to the classroom: Robert Fanning, dressing in a disheveled wig and wacky glasses, speaking with a French accent and convincing his students that he was Mr. Fanning's long-lost twin, Dr. Miles Tugot, who had come to fill in for the day as Mr. Fanning journeyed to the distant continents of the imagination. I'll not soon forget Jamaal May, wearing pink bunny ears along with otherwise cool attire for a seventh grade classroom at Clippert Academy, where, at the end of the year, he would confer his "Brickheart Awards"—hearts made of Legos—as prizes for the bravest student poems. Dr. Suzanne Scarfone, who opens each class with ritual chimes and chanted poems to introduce her "Poetry Palace"—a special artistic realm of peace, gentle behavior, and imagination that one year evolved into "Ringer of the Moon," an original opera created and performed at the Detroit Opera House by the third and fourth grade Poets of her "Poetry Palace." Anita Schmaltz in full clown regalia at her school's year-end gala, encouraging a gifted third grader with a severe speech impediment to belt out his poem, meanwhile pointing to an easel chart with his words writ large so the rest of the children could follow along.

Aricka Foreman, Isaac Miller, and Chace Morris bring the courage and social justice commitment of poetry slam—they have won awards from Women of the World, Brave New Voices, and the Rust Belt Slam, respectively—to iO classrooms and Citywide Poets sites after school. Aricka and Isaac coached Citywide Poets 2011 Brave New Voices National Youth Poetry Slam team to 4th place—in the *world*—as they performed in the finals before an audience of 3,000 at the San Francisco Opera House, rousing their audience and triumphing over issues such as domestic abuse, gender discrimination, violence, and racism. Julia Putnam's passion for social justice and education has led her to establish an entire school—the Jimmie and Grace Lee Boggs Educational Center, dedicated to nurturing creativity and critical thought and cultivating the souls of children and the community that surrounds them. I'm proud that such a pioneering educator gained some of her first classroom experiences through iO.

Nandi Comer, who was a ninth grader and one of my students in the first official iO class in 1995 at Communication and Media Arts High School, worked as writer-in-residence and then iO Community Projects Coordinator after earning her BA from the University of Michigan. She expanded Citywide Poets (CWP), involving our youth in spoken-word programs outside of Detroit, and creating summer poetry and public art workshops for youth. She oversaw the annual CWP anthologies and directed CWP's participation in an intergenerational poetry and story workshop, "Boomtown," in conjunction with Matrix Theatre and the University of Michigan.

*Terry Blackhawk*

Kristin Palm picked up the CWP baton in 2001 when administering iO demanded more of my attention. The program involves intense mentorship, camaraderie, and artistic discipline as youth learn performance and writing skills and take their performances to venues in Detroit and beyond. After Kristin moved to California, CWP languished. Nandi re-established this program, helping us to reach hundreds of wonderful young people, giving them the tools to face life with courage and confidence and, again, tell the world who they are. The CWP program became strong enough that iO received a National Youth Programming in the Arts and the Humanities Award (formerly "Coming Up Taller") conferred by Michelle Obama at the White House in 2009. I had started Citywide Poets in 1998, once iO had moved out of my third bedroom and into our first office in the Palms Building opposite Detroit's Comerica Park. I met with students on the tenth floor, as the setting sun spread across the city's rooftops, in a corner room whose ambience is so aptly captured by Lena Cintron in the poem below.

**Tenth Floor, Left Corner**
(poetry class)

Bare shaven camera heads
like film exposed. Green nails
on small hands. From the deep
crevices of cold sparkly purses,
wasted bits of paper full
of words too powerful to fit
their allotted space kiss
tiny notebooks (moleskines)
that cost more
than the expensive cup
of coffee needed to fill them.

Discarded gloves left
by the tableside to make
room for anxious fingers

that grip pens like oars
in a boat rushing to shore.

This is poetry's womb.

I'm proud that this poem was chosen for presentation at the Kennedy Center during the Coming Up Taller awards reception the evening before we went to the White House. Matthew Olzmann was Lena's CWP instructor for several years, in that same room, and with her, as with all his students, from elementary through high school, he conveyed wit and willingness to be surprised. It was Matthew who conferred upon me what became the title of this introduction: "Patron Saint of the Soundless Gears." It came to him one September during our annual writers' orientation, when we broke out in pairs to share and assign one another names, based on writing about objects in the Detroit Children's Museum. Matthew and I were partners, and I had chosen a Rube Goldberg–like sculpture to write about, hence the gears. I'm not sure what name I gave to him. I'm pretty sure it had something to do with baseball, about which he is quite passionate, but it was not nearly so imaginative and memorable as his gift to me.

Recently I was talking with Lannan Literary Fellow Jamaal May, who was back in Detroit after a fellowship at Bucknell University and touring with his award-winning first book of poems, *Hum*. He and I were discussing the concept of windows, and, as the architect of iO, I've been giving windows some thought. A while back, while leading a workshop with a group of teachers, I had us all create metaphors for ourselves as teachers. Many saw themselves as various kinds of leaders—lion tamers, engineers on trains, symphony conductors, movie producers—but the metaphor that came to me was window. And the image has stayed with me, as a medium through whom energy, information, light, learning all pass. I guess that's why it resonates with *educare*, the Latin root for education, meaning to educe, draw forth that which is within, and that's why I like Matt's "soundless gears." The fact that iO has grown as well as it has is often a marvel to me, and I credit many things for buoying us up throughout the years. A window, I realize, is not exactly the best image for a leader. It doesn't help to create plans or specify goals and objectives. But it does allow for vision, and it's happy when the things around it share their light.

Along with the writers who have inhabited this beautiful house, there are others, some no longer with us, living presences that take up residence with iO. I speak here of poets, of the poets of all ages, living and dead, whose souls live through their words, and I especially love that "stanza" in Italian means "room." Read through these essays and you will gather a reading list of poets whose words can sustain you and whose stanzas you will want to wander through. So I give credit to poetry itself for being part of the lifeblood of iO, and I also give credit to the good will and generosity of the people of Detroit—educators, families, parents, writers, friends—and of course, most of all, to the children themselves, who year after year, in the words of Good Brother Markus, "open their great big hearts and let us in."

Big-heartedness, bedrock, caring, truth, roses, hugs, community. Shirley Bolden, the quintessential student. Mr. Eric, the quintessential caring teacher. The principal. The EWI ladies whose altruism makes the world a better place. These are the elements of iO and these are also the elements of Detroit. As the national spotlight trains ever more on Detroit and everyone seems to have an opinion about our city, these essays cast an eye on the dynamic relationships between writers and Detroit students, and they give an intimate look into our youths' concerns. It's been my opinion for a long time now that iO is unique among similar programs around the country in that the city itself is a character in our students' lives and in their writing. Detroit is a city that has struggled with identity and self-definition and re-self-definition more than others, and I'm sure we could fill more than one anthology of poems by youth defining their city. From public art to ruin porn to sociological treatises, everyone else seems to be claiming or defining Detroit these days. I want to let our kids have a say as well.

The images of the city served up by iO students over the years could wrap more than a few buildings in downtown Detroit. For

Joshua, "Detroit is a downtrodden woman / and she is crying right now / her tears reflecting the lost skyline / the glamour and jazz." Richard is from "mac & cheese and homemade pie / broken porches and board windows / from loud mouths and comedy / from bloody knuckles and closed fists." Rashad warns, "Cars whip past. What you asking for? / You better keep your mouth closed / You don't want to end up a victim of Joy Road."

That our young people give voice to the frustrations of growing up in stark urban settings should not come as a surprise. But they also play with the material they are given. Marie wants to "dance / in the intersection of / Dequindre and Seven Mile / to silent music." For Naidra, "Nicholas Cage is Detroit in leather pants / whining over spilled metaphors . . . / dancing to music / of the homeless man with gray eyes . . . / singing spirituals on the People / Mover / volunteering at the soup kitchen / paving broken roads . . ." And they find comfort. Fourth grader Jonathan's father "is like a bodyguard to me / the shooting star in the middle of the night / a house that protects me from the rain / the dog that loves me no matter what / the map that leads me to my destination."

iO students sing of their hopes for the future and their own role in it, with a sense that they can make the future happen. Eighth grader Mario is "The king bee out of the hive / The brain of Martin Luther King, Jr. / The Obama of my neighborhood / The treasure of the chest." Finally, Citywide Poets' Joseph Verge shows us the beauty in his city's resilience in this poem that he wrote and then performed for a Detroit Institute of Arts photography exhibit "Detroit Revealed" in 2012.

**Taking Root**
In Southwest Detroit
Life grows best on the roofs of abandoned buildings.
Outsiders look at the graffiti juxtaposed against islands of grass
but don't understand that art and science create wonders.
When I moved near Vernor St.
it took me a while to blend in with the community.
Like oil paint submerged in water, I always stood out.

Maybe I never understood the environment.
Learning the culture was like trying to decode
the meaning of a Van Gogh painting,
except my neighborhood was more like a mosaic
of different backgrounds glued together by struggle,
to prove that those abandoned buildings aren't abandoned.

Our city's hopes live there, like dandelions
yawning beneath the sun on Sunday morning.
They grow on city roads and in schoolyards,
on the surface of children's minds,
in the hearts of people who've been left behind
by everyone else. But they stand tall, their wild hair
blowing seeds of change across the horizon,
taking root in places they were told they'd never grow.

My dandelions have been the poets who've shown
me that weeds can be beautiful in their resilience,
that everything planted won't choke the sunlight out,
that just because they get overlooked doesn't
mean they don't exist.

They learn to adapt,
refuse to die quietly beneath
the ruin.

When I founded InsideOut in the mid 1990s, the burgeoning creative writing movement, industry, community—call it what you will—was beginning to take off, but I could not have imagined the reach that is has today. From a handful of writers in 1990, attendance at annual conferences of the flagship professional organization for creative writers and creative writing programs—the AWP (Association of Writers and Writing Programs)—was beginning to grow. There were 4,000 attendees in 2004. The 2014 AWP conference in Seattle hosted 13,000 writers; and, from seventy-odd college creative writing programs across the country in the mid-1970s, we now see 880. Initially AWP did not serve K–12 programs. iO participated in a caucus of Writers in the Schools programs, meeting for several years as an off-site "guerrilla" group, until we became a recognized partner within AWP, and I was privileged to be the first representative of the national Writers in the Schools alliance on the AWP board. The WITS Alliance, which consisted of about half a dozen core groups in 1998, is also growing and now has over 30 allied organizations and regularly fields requests from writers and community activists who are eager to start more. Like other WITS programs, we at iO take pride in the excellent credentials of the writers who serve in our Detroit classrooms. Along with AWP, we believe that the art of writing is essential to a good education, and skilled practitioners, i.e., literary role models, are essential to its success. I look forward to the day when we can have a poet in every school. As MFA programs in creative writing continue to proliferate and talented writers look for meaningful, engaging work, it's not too extreme to think that this might be a possibility.

I hope that this anthology will offer a marker in the history of this movement and meaningful insights into what makes our work, as Emily Dickinson said of her poems, "breathe." It's heartening that iO has flourished for so long. As for-profit enterprises increasingly encroach on education, InsideOut's mission to empower young people to "think broadly, create bravely, and share their voices with the wider world" becomes ever more important. Programs like Inside-Out, which foster voice, independent thinking, and self-expression, help young people to build the competence and resilience necessary to face a challenging world. On a recent NPR interview, iO Citywide Poet Terrell Morrow explained how poetry has helped him to see the world and his place in it more clearly. "When you grow up in the city, you become an adult a lot quicker than most people. I just started writing poetry two years ago, and I'm really opening up to a broader vision and seeing how we can affect the world. I have more pride in my city as opposed to before. I've come to see there's beauty in everything . . . there's so much inspiration. Just to take hold of that. It's something that's coming."

# How to Turn an Ordinary Floor into an Oceanside Beach with One Hand

*Field Notes Concerning the Precise Location of the Imagination*

Matthew Olzmann

> *All third graders are surrealists, saboteurs, reckless, ready to plunge into the deepest abyss, laughing.*
> Dean Young, *The Art of Recklessness*

Let's start with an annoying conversation.

AWP 2012: The hotel bar is crowded, because the hotel bar is always crowded. At one table, writers are drinking and swearing and laughing and arguing. The argument is about "pedagogy" and the value of creative writing programs, but really it's an intense display of intellectual one-upmanship. One writer says one thing, and the other—as if on cue—immediately disagrees. They dance back and forth like this until the person arguing "against" the value of writing programs blurts out, "Yeah? Well, you can't teach imagination, can you?"

The conversation fizzles out after this, the air is released as if from some grand balloon. People pay their tabs. It's late. This is boring.

Here's a conversation that haunts me. In the winter in 2007, I was a visiting artist for a middle school in Southwest Detroit. This wasn't for InsideOut (though I had been working there as well and had been for several years). This was during a time when I was always working two or three part-time jobs while finishing up college and beginning grad school, and I was grateful for this extra opportunity. I was to meet with a class of eighth graders once a week for eight weeks.

One week, a kid says to me, "I don't know if I can write poems."

"What makes you say that?"

"Because I don't have an imagination."

"Sure you do. Everyone does."

"Not me."

"Yes. Even you. I'm sure. Look at all the drawings you make." His drawings were impressive. He had entire notebooks filled.

But he didn't seem convinced. He said, "Can you teach me how to have an imagination?"

"I don't have to teach you; you already have one."

"Well, if I have an imagination, how do I find it?"

Then the bell rang. "We'll work on this," I told him as the class gathered their gear and began filing out. I left the school feeling a sense of resolve. Next week: we're talking about the imagination.

I had a mission.

But there wouldn't be a next week for him. His teacher called me, just days later, and said he'd been shot. He opened the door to his house to let in a friend who was running from trouble. Someone opened fire. And that's how abruptly this part of the story ends.

About four years before that, I worked my first residency for Inside-Out. A high school. First day: nothing but awesomeness. Students were enthusiastic, even if only because writing poems meant they didn't have to be writing essays. They had escaped from the jaws of "real" schoolwork.

Here's a conversation that baffled me. I had just given the "assignment" and students were digging in to write their poems. Then, a tentative hand raised near the back of the room.

"Yes?" I said.

"Does this poem need a thesis?" she asked.

Then another student raised her hand: "And how many paragraphs does this need to be?"

I guess they hadn't escaped the essay after all.

The first time I worked with students who weren't teenagers was at Lessenger K–8. By this time, I'd been with InsideOut for maybe eight years. For this residency, I'd have a seventh grade class, an eighth grade class, and a third grade class. *Third grade*? What was I supposed to do with that? I was dreading walking into that classroom, but when I got there something amazing happened. They were discussing what they wanted to be when they grew up. It went like this:

"I want to be doctor."

"I want to be president."

"I want to be a dolphin."

There was a smattering of giggles, and I thought that last comment would dislodge the room's tenuous attention. Instead, it crystalized it. The room was now energized, orbiting that impossible aspiration like some bright, new star.

"No! *I* want to be a dolphin!"

"I want to be a dolphin, too!"

"Well, I want to be a dragon!"

"Well, I want live on the moon!"

Whatever happened was instantaneous. One after another, whatever possessed the first student to declare her desire to be a dolphin rippled through the room. It was contagious. And soon, this room—that only seconds ago wanted to be doctors and politicians—was filled with future dolphins and space monsters.

These conversations are all out of order. The four scenes I just presented occurred independently of each other over the span of about a decade. It's like one of those pictures where you can't see anything when you're standing up close, but take a few steps back and an image blooms into view.

Only now, looking back from a distance, can I see that these four moments are absolutely connected. One leads to the next leads to the next. Consider the lifespan of the human imagination.

- 3rd grade. It's alive and thriving. *I want to be a dolphin.*
- 8th grade. It's doubting itself. *If I have an imagination, how do I find it?*
- 12th grade. It arrives in critical condition. Sirens are going off now. It needs immediate medical attention, or it risks fading completely from view. *Does this poem need a thesis? How many paragraphs does this need to be?*
- Then the MFA graduates and professors at a bar at AWP. *You can't teach imagination, can you?* Now, the imagination is be-

ing revised out of having ever existed in the first place. It's declared to be domain of the privileged. It's some rare blood type that only the lucky or gifted are born with. Everyone else never had it, and it can't be taught to them. They are doomed to boring lives of infomercials and Reality TV.

You can see the decline, and it's frightening to think what comes next.

*A kid says to me, "I don't know if I can write poems."*
  *"What makes you say that?"*
  *"Because I don't have an imagination."*
  *"Sure you do. Everyone does."*
Did I say this conversation haunts me? Because it does. I wrestled with it for years afterward. Maybe, it's simply the spotlight of tragedy where everything is illuminated, magnified, and eternal. When I said, "Everyone has an imagination," I believed that, and still do. Every kid who once played cops and robbers, who had a conversation with a stuffed animal, or threw a basketball toward a hoop pretending it was Game Seven of the NBA Finals has an imagination.

That's not opinion. That's fact. It's something anyone can prove by falling asleep and dreaming.

It's the next part of the conversation that gives me trouble.
  *"Well, if I have an imagination, how do I find it?"*
That's the real question. How do you access the imagination once it's been buried by peer pressure and the desire to grow up and be taken seriously? How do you reclaim it once it's been drained by scantrons or schools that lay off their art teachers or cities that consider selling the contents of their museums?

What could I have told him?

Where could he have begun to look?

Here's a final scene. My last year with InsideOut—before a job in another state took me out of town—I did a residency at Cooke Elementary. There I worked with another third grade class. There's a writing exercise I got from Pete Markus (InsideOut's Senior Writer and Language-Magician-in-Residence). It involves looking at your hand and saying all the things it can do. *My hand can play piano. My hand can turn on the TV.* Now, let's think of all the things you *wish* your hand could do. Touch the stars. Turn rocks into puppies. Let's call this your "dream hand." Write about it.

Here's an example from Kalila Mason-Smith:

**What My Dream Hand Can Do**
My dream hand can
make me fly. When I
make a fist, I can
become the best skater.
When I wave my hand,
I become famous. When I make
my hand bang on the table,
ice and snowballs come out.
When I open and close my
hand, I can get a hovercraft
or flying machine.

Have you ever seen thirty kids all holding their hands in front of their faces and staring as if their hands were foreign objects? As if their fingers had arrived from another planet? Remember how I was saying imagination at this age is contagious? How if one kid wants to be a dolphin, then the next wants to be a dragon?

That's how the dream hand works.

Suddenly, you have hands that are made of fire, hands that travel through time, hands that turn math books into Xboxes, hands that lift mountains, and hands that speak to the dead.

*"If I have an imagination, how do I find it?"*

Before a kid reaches the age where he has to ask that question, the imagination is everywhere. Could I have told him that? Look everywhere? It's all places? It is literally in your own two hands? It seems far-fetched, but when I think of those kids at Cooke Elementary, it also seems very possible.

Look at them. They lift their palms up to the light. They wave and shake their hands with fury. They tap their fingers on their desks and consider the sounds that the desks make in response. They hold their hands way out, stretch their arms as far as they can reach, then they bring them in real close to examine their palms, their fists, their knuckles, their fingernails as if the heart of the Earth is there—alive, new, and suddenly visible.

# What Color Is in Between?

*Poetry and Creative Vision in Children*

*Norene Cashen*

A child looks up at the full moon and sees vanilla ice cream or a snowball thrown to the sky by a giant. In my elementary school classrooms, we refer to this as wearing our "poetry glasses" because we recognize that poetry is not only an art form—it's also a way of seeing, one that comes very naturally to a child.

Before children even hear the term *metaphor* or *simile*, inventive comparisons are part of life, present in both work and play. They're already using these literary devices in order to map and organize the world. *This thimble is a tiny hat. That potato looks like a human head.* Children are experts at making unexpected leaps that link one thing to another.

That's why, given freedom, inspiration, and a few good poetry prompts, children adapt quickly to composing lines that reflect intensity and wisdom far beyond their years. I remember a fourth grader who wrote a poem that begins, "I am a lost balloon." In the second line of the poem, he says, "I push myself." Suddenly, it isn't the force of nature or physics that moves the balloon upward into space. It's the sheer will of the speaker, who also confesses to his wish to be loved, to travel to Paris, to be near the sea, and to be in the hands of a child. By the end of the poem, there's a crash, a descent into the idea that this kind of longing and vulnerability can only end tragically. "I am alone," the speaker says in the final lines. "I feel destroyed."

The first thing I try to teach children in a workshop isn't rhyme or alliteration. It's the importance and power of their inherent creative vision. Albert Einstein might have agreed with my teaching priorities, as he once said, "The true sign of intelligence is not knowledge but imagination."

Every connection a child makes births a new meaning with nuances and contexts that can't always be standardized or fully understood in a literal sense. The particular objects and images they choose are unique to their experiences and the mysterious inner processes they use to understand the world. That's what gives their poems—expressions that don't need to be understood literally—substance and a deeper kind of truth.

In the school setting, the acquisition of knowledge is dominant. So in order to write amazing poems, we have to establish a different value system and an alternative set of guidelines for our workshops. Creativity and courage take priority over rules and correctness. The objective is to tap into our inner voices instead of funneling information from the outside.

In the early stages of my school residencies, I've seen children so gripped by the fear of making a spelling mistake they can't move their pencils. They need reassurance and encouragement to put the first few words on the page. I remind them that, in poetry, there is no right or wrong. As we say in the classroom, "The only way to get it wrong is to not do it at all." For some children, poetry is also an act of bravery that helps them to overcome a lack of confidence and its accompanying inhibitions.

I teach every workshop under the overarching idea that imagination is the thing we must explore, nurture, honor, and take pride in. It's the tool we pick up and use to make great art. All children can learn to trust it, and in doing so, learn to trust themselves.

Even though I'm the one teaching these workshops week after week, I'm still surprised by the quality and depth of poems written by children. When I take home a stack of writing folders, I often marvel at the beautiful outcomes I find there. Each successful poem is proof that poetry is an active conduit between a child's mysterious inner world and the outer world.

In 2009, Naivit Morales, another fourth grade student of mine at Bennett Elementary School, wrote this modified haiku:

The sky is blue
The ocean is blue
What color is in between?

I was immediately struck by its profound, authoritative voice. This tiny poem seemed to crack open a new space in the image of sky and ocean by placing the idea of some unknown color between the two. To this day, I have that haiku memorized. Along with some of my favorite lines by famous poets like Emily Dickinson and Walt Whitman, I recite it regularly in workshops and conversations about writing.

The fact that Naivit's poem made such a significant impact on me as a writer and teacher is more evidence of the magic that happens when poetry meets imagination in children. In three brief lines, her poem did some of the most important work a poem can do. It asked me to look at the world in a completely new way and invited me to see something in the skyline that never existed before, not until she dared to put those words on the page.

# In the Dream

*Robert Fanning*

"What did you do with Duane?"

I remember her words distinctly, and what seemed her accusatory tone. I remember the lump in my throat. She was one of the tougher teachers at Hutchins Middle School, a kind but stern woman, and not one whose classroom I worked in. And now she was standing before me—a rookie InsideOut writer-in-residence—in the busy hallway among the cacophony of kids and bells and book bags.

"What did I do with Duane?" I stammered in reply, not quite knowing what she meant.

I did know immediately the student to whom she was referring because I'd seen her chewing him out on more than one occasion. Duane was, in the eyes of some of his teachers, a handful, a troublemaker, one who won't sit still. Indeed, many days he posed challenges for me in the classroom, too. He couldn't keep his hands to himself. He'd always have an excuse to be sharpening and re-sharpening his pencil or just walking around; he'd nudge a girl with his elbow, jostle a boy's backpack, accidentally knock someone's notebook off their desk. Most days, I'd let him draw, or just be. I'd ask him to keep his hands to himself, but let him do whatever he wanted while the rest of us wrote poems. I could tell Duane was interested in what we were writing. He was curious. But for whatever reason, he'd always stay in the shadow just beyond the penumbra of our fire.

The day we decided to talk about memories, his face lit up. Our memory is like a great big box in our chest, I told the students that day. It is filled with things. With ice-cream cones, birthday candles. With shouting. With falling off our bike the first time. Some days that box is filled with happy times, and other days it is filled with pain, but for us poets it is always a treasure box.

That morning, I saw Duane's pen moving, his eyes intent on the page, his teeth gnawing on his lower lip in bravery and concentration. And with the simple prompt to make a list poem beginning with the words "I remember . . ." or " I remember the day . . ." he wrote this:

**The Memory I Remember**
I remember the day
my mom died.
I was so mad I cried.
I was in the bathroom
and my tooth was loose.
I heard my mom
say I am going out . . .
Then I turned around
and my tooth fell out.
I came out of the bathroom
and ran to the car
and she pulled off.
I never got to show her
my tooth.

Duane pushed the paper aside when he was done. There was more to it, five or so other lines after the last one that changed the subject. The next week, Duane listened carefully as I kneeled beside him and we talked about where the poem seemed to really end. I did not tell Duane that his poem was as fierce and pure a shard as a poem can get and that when I read it, multiple times, the air left my gut and tears streamed down my cheeks. The edges of Duane's lips were curling upward as he talked about his poem. He already knew its power. I didn't need to tell him.

That next week's class discussion was about dreams, and the kids were thrilled, as we all are, to share some of the wild dreams they've had—their flying dreams, their video-game dreams, their silly dreams. I worried we would run out of time to write because there were so many hands up—so many kids wanting to outdo each other describing the landscape of their wacky and sometimes frightening dream world. When it came time to write about dreams—one of my possible prompts was geared toward those children who might not remember a good dream to write about. This prompt was: Write a poem imagining another person's (or animal's) dream, by completing this title: In the Dream of _____.

As the students all began to write and the room grew charged with the quiet lightning of poetry, Duane raised his hand and asked if his title could be "In the Dream of Dead People." A few kids chuckled, no doubt assuming he was joking. I said: That is a great idea, Duane. And this is what he wrote:

**In The Dream of Dead People**
In the dream of dead people,
they are talking to you
and walking around.
Some of the dead people
are dancing and having
a good time on the dance floor.
Dead people are your legal guardians.
They help you if you need it or not.
Dead people are telling jokes
and laughing. They are driving
you to school and driving
you back home. Some are
having so much fun,
their bones are falling apart.

I know the old desert island question is so worn out, but in considering what poems I would bring with me for company on such a lonely oasis, I would think by now, after some thirty years that I'd have a truckload of such poems. The fact is, I only have a box full. Keats's "Ode to Autumn." Whitman's *Leaves of Grass*. One by Stanley Kunitz. A handful by Plath. A handful by Dylan Thomas. A dozen or so from Merwin's *Second Four Books of Poems*. And the rest would be a large stack of poems by contemporary poets, many of whom are friends from my time at InsideOut. But right near the top of that small box of poems would be this poem, "In the Dream of Dead People," by Duane, from Hutchins Middle School.

I have carried this poem with me for these past thirteen years, and I will carry it with me until, well, until I'm shaking my dead bones on some dance floor. I have shared it with dozens of friends and poets over the years, and continue to share it with my students at Central Michigan University, where I teach now. It is one of those rare diamonds that shines just as bright every time I look at it.

Duane's poem is deeply heartrending, especially following the poem that preceded it the week before. However, look more closely at its achievement. The poem is in second person, thereby bringing the reader into its focus, into its dream. And who is having this dream? The Dead. Following the huge leap of courage in writing about his mother's death, Duane now—only a week later—enters the world of the collective Dead, into their very living dream. In this dream, Dead People still dance and laugh. There is a lot of hoopla in their world; they party, they rattle their skeletons on the dance floor. However, it is easy to see what's almost literally between the lines here; the Dead People are not only "having a good time . . ." they continue also to love and to parent: "They are your legal guardians. / They help you if you need it or not . . . / They are driving you to school and driving you back home." Dead People are, it seems, kept alive in this poem and this dream, and in the heart of this author: by their very connection to us, the living, their children.

The end of this poem is, like the endings of the best poems, never-ending. It is an ever-outward pulse of light: "Some are / having so much fun, / their bones are falling apart." Here, my God—only by going on an instant journey through his own subconscious pain and fear—this boy, Duane, this young poet, this brave seer—finds joy, finds celebration, finds laughter despite loss and beyond death, by bridging the distance between the living and the dead. In the poem's great final scene, this dance of the dead that allows them to shake loose their very bones, Duane, as a poet, transcends both life and death. He goes straight to the current of light between worlds, allowing both the Dead People and us, the Living People, who witness this dance of a poem, this miracle, to be more alive.

Several weeks after Duane wrote this poem, and several others, I was looking this seemingly angry teacher in the eye, not knowing how to answer.

"Yes, that's what I said. What did you do with Duane?" She repeated her question, smiling now.

"Duane was on my 'to be kicked out of school list' and now he's one of my best students, and I think it's because of the poetry . . ." She went on to tell me how it was the talk of the teacher's lounge, how mature and kind Duane had become, how focused he'd become on his schoolwork.

In all the hubbub of the end of that school day, I never had a chance to respond to this teacher's question. But what I would have liked to say is: I didn't do anything with Duane, except maybe show him to a door in himself he needed to open, the way poetry does, and that's at the core of the mission of InsideOut Literary Arts Project. Duane was not only bursting with utterly nuclear creativity that needed an outlet—as so many kids—and humans—are, he was also swirling with confusion; he was being carried in a river of pain and needed the time to be inward, a chance for the transformative power of language to carry him to calmer water. I don't know if we're even meant to sit still for long in this life, any of us, really, but certainly not children, and especially not when we've lost someone we love, especially a parent.

I have no doubt poetry allowed Duane to look beyond the frantic tongues of that fire in himself and to find its energy, its healing power. And maybe he only needed these poems. Many InsideOut students can't get enough of the power of poetry when they find it—they become leaders in the classroom, they look for other experiences in the organization, they become Citywide Poets as teens, they shine into adulthood as poets. Maybe all Duane needed was these poems, this one experience—but it changed him, utterly and outwardly. He became, by this experience, a different person. Duane is just one student of literally dozens who I personally watched undergo this transformation of survival, of joy, of immeasurable inner knowing—when shown the fire of language, the torch of poetry. And with his torch held high, and with this poem he found deep within himself, Duane's courage continually reminds me how to survive, how to live.

# Conduit: Connecting All the Stampeding Hearts

*Jamaal May*

## Pomegranate Means Grenade

> *The heart trembles like a herd of horses.*
> Jontae McCrory—age 11

Hold a pomegranate in your palm.
Imagine ways to split it. Think of the breaking
skin as shrapnel. Remember granada
means pomegranate and granada
means grenade because grenade
takes its name from the fruit;
identify war by what it takes away
from fecund orchards. Jontae,
these are the arms they will fear from you.
There will always be at least one like you:
a child who gets the picked-over box
with mostly black crayons. One who wonders
what beautiful has to do with beauty as he darkens
a sun in the corner of every page,
constructs a house from ashen lines,
sketches stick figures lying face down—
I know how often red is the only color
left to reach for. I fear for you.
My heart trembles like a herd of horses.
You are writing a stampede into my chest.
This is the same thumping anxiety that shudders
me when I push past marines in high school
hallways, moments after their video footage
of young men dropping from helicopters
in night vision goggles. I want you to see
in the dark without covering your face,
carry verse as countermeasure to recruitment videos,

and remember the cranes buried inside poems
that hung in Tiananmen Square—
remember because Huang Xiang was exiled
for these, exiled for this, the calligraphy of revolt.
You stand nameless in front of a tank against
those who would rather see you pull a pin
from a grenade than pull a pen
from your backpack. Jontae,
they are afraid.

JAMAAL MAY

In the photograph the man smiles and waves. A sun smiles on his bandana and banners wave behind him. This shot, captured in Tiananmen Square, took place just before the tanks rolled in and the much more famous picture from that era was snapped. The man in the photo is the father of the college student who began to tremble and weep while explaining to me how moved she was by a poem I'd just read, "Pomegranate Means Grenade." I stepped from behind the table and did what felt most natural: I hugged her. I held her until I could feel her weeping through my shirt and against my skin, then held on until her short gasps for air slowed and she repeated, "Thank you."

Her father was not unlike the poet invoked in "Pomegranate Means Grenade," Huang Xiang, a writer, calligrapher, and activist for human rights and free speech. Both stood up to the government, both survived and eventually made their way to the United States, Xiang being imprisoned by the Communist Chinese government a dozen times along the way. The college student said she was continuously troubled by the reality of those who suffer in the fight for free expression. Knowing her father could have died that day makes the Tiananmen Square massacre more than a historical footnote to her and made the poem that much more important in her eyes.

I needed the poem that night to help me remember why creating and sharing was vital. This college reading was my first featured appearance after a six-month bout with stage fright that kept me from taking readings I couldn't afford to pass up financially. I grappled with the possibility that I would never again be able to stand in front of an audience and recite what I had written. "Pomegranate Means Grenade" was a necessary poem in my push to break the spell of defeat. It always connects me to something larger, something more important than my own sense of comfort.

"Pomegranate Means Grenade" was written in the summer after my first year of working with the InsideOut Literary Arts Project. The poem was inspired by students there who were so open and brilliant and creative, I couldn't help but fear for the safety of their spirits. It opens with an epigraph from one such student, Jontae McCrory, an eleven-year-old, who, on the first day of class, raised his hand and asked if I read Lord Byron. Throughout the year Jontae showed an attention to language and love for fresh metaphor and imagery that was astonishing. "The heart trembles like a herd of horses," writes Jontae in his poem "Burning Soul." Here is the poem in its entirety.

> The burning soul of the spiritual part
> of a human being that is believed
> to survive death opens
> like a thousand roses in mid-spring
>
> and the ash of the phoenix
> that burns like one thousand suns.
>
> The burning sore,
> like the sting of a wasp.
>
> The heart trembles
> like a herd of horses.
>
> Scars the soul like ten stab wounds.
>
> The linking of newborn blood.

When I first read "The heart trembles / like a herd of horses," I wished I had written those lines. The idea of a trembling heart hints to weakness while the herd of horses projects power. This paradox is a fruitful way to approach life; with a heart that is vulnerable but has the power to shake the earth. One of the many things I learned from working with these students was this lesson about the real power of vulnerability. To truly write to the core of human experience I have to be at least as exposed as the hearts of children. Emotionally connected writing demands no less.

The linking that occurs at the end of "Burning Soul" has resonated with me for years and keeps opening like those spring roses. I've come to think of what Jontae implies as connection between death and rebirth ("newborn blood") as being representative of another, related conduit—the one that connects us all in something like a cultural ecosystem. Because we cannot truly know one another's minds we need conduits for closer understanding, a meeting place between one mind and another. Art can serve as this conduit, specifically in this case, the art of creative writing.

William Carlos Williams famously wrote, "No ideas but in things," first in the poem "A Sort of a Song" then repeatedly in the long poem "Patterson." This basic tenet of the Imagist movement has continued to influence contemporary poetry, and it serves as an excellent aid in explaining this concept of creating conduits with poems. When someone says "longing," nothing is conjured in the mind, so therefore the writer and reader, also other readers of the same word, are not sharing a mental experience. When the writer says "red wheelbarrow," we are sharing the image of that particular thing. It's not the exact image, but we are all closer. All communication is approximation at best. By expressing ideas through objects, using symbolism, juxtaposition, metaphor, etc., we can manufacture a liminal space that is a closer approximation of the same ideas. This is how we connect to each other through words. This is at the core of the transformative power of literature.

Considering how this all functions on the micro level, it is no surprise then that a poem written by an eleven-year-old in Detroit eventually united an emotionally broken performer and a haunted college student four years later and six hundred miles away. The catharsis of that moment is only one of the many conduit paths I can trace back from my experiences in the classroom. That same year dozens of other poets in Detroit connected with thousands of other students through the InsideOut Literary Arts Project. Take into account twenty years of this kind of life-changing work and it becomes impossible to argue the value of InsideOut and organizations like it who inspire the newborn blood to create tomorrow's literature today, challenging all trembling hearts to shake the ground with hoofbeats.

# The Poet as Empathetic Witness

*Suzanne Scarfone*

At 10:30 on a cloudy Tuesday morning, bafflement clouds the faces of these third graders as they watch, warily, a grown woman talking about moons and stars and music, asking them to close their eyes and drift on a stream of consciousness. Skepticism abounds. What are you? Who are you? What are you talking about? I don't see water rolling by my desk. When is recess? What time is it? I'm hungry. I'm thirsty. I want my mother.

I am the poet in front of the room, the grown woman who believes in uncovering the sense of wonder buried beneath the surface. Soon, the initial comfort dissolves, and quiet settles over the drab schoolroom. One by one, boys and girls surrender, some reluctantly, to the calm of sound, the music of Debussy, then embrace it. Maybe this poet person is telling us the truth. The music does sound like something, like pictures. Mmmm. Sounds make pictures. Sounds make poetry. Poetry makes me feel, makes me see, makes me want to play, dance.

Malik collects his musical pictures and cradles the words in his eyes like soft souls. "We are in a museum making music," he writes. "Happy song / nice song / up and down." Bunched together in the back row, two girls, best friends, sway to the rhythm. Up front, curious and unsure, three boys embark on this journey together and pour out a song of celebration. "We are coming in the world / How are you doing my world? / You are like a windy song." Over in the third row, Anthony, a loner, hurriedly scrawls: "I will raise to the sky / so I can open my soul to the poetry of my life and yours forever."

The music crescendos. A desk shakes, as Marquise writes forcefully about his quest. He is swimming in "waves of change" and "fighting for freedom." He writes to set his reader on "a mission, a journey, out in the world. . . . Get the sword of the wind water," he exhorts, before bidding "Farewell!"

In the middle of the room, Koi whispers to me that she feels like heaven is everywhere in a garden of imagination. "In the garden I have on blue like the clouds / The sun is smiling at me / When I smile, I hear the clouds talking in sweet voices." Next to her, the dreamer, Tatianna, finds in the music a way to free herself of a secret fear: "Tell me, girl, why are you sad? / You're staring at the wall of memories. / Are you thinking about your mother dying? or your father? / or is your fairy godmother gone?"

Over the years, teaching with InsideOut Literary Arts Project has shown me that poetry is a healing art. My poetry is full of hope. My poems find power and joy everywhere, even in the midst of loss and disenfranchisement. I desire to give space in each of my works to the strange beauty found in the everyday. They give hope to me and to the vulnerable, to the silenced with whom I work.

As a writer-in-residence for thirteen years, I have found strength in digging deep inside to create the visions that will make our world an equitable and joyful place in which to live. Magically, by the end of classes like the one above, the flow of sounds and words creates a sanctuary from the jarring buzz of school bells—a sea of spirit and joy. We also create a place of safety and acceptance. Along with my Detroit students, I know that delving into the messy, emotional, and sometimes painful considerations of self-love, of love of others and of family and of forgiveness brings power, pleasure, and a sense of belonging to all of us.

Over the years, my teaching has become increasingly based on the premise that a central way to help heal the wounds caused by racism, war, sexism, poverty, and hopelessness is to touch one student at a time, bonding one writer to another writer, thus bringing together many. In my InsideOut classes, empathy has turned out to be the key to the power of healing. I believe that empathy empowers through hope those who have been made to feel invisible, and I marvel at the desperate longing and gritty realism that prompts my students to put lips on words sweet enough to reveal their souls, capture their landscapes, and reform their worlds.

Concurrent with my most recent assignment as an iO writer-in-residence, I have worked as a poetry mentor with the Afghan Women's Writing Project, which establishes online, virtual classrooms led by women authors in order to give Afghan girls and women the freedom to express themselves. Each Afghan writer risks her life because of her involvement in these writing workshops, but although the Taliban have mutilated, raped, thrown acid at, and stoned those who dare to write the truth of their condition, the women persevere. I have brought the writings of these Afghan writers into my middle school classrooms on Detroit's east side. There my students have read poems, stories, and essays in which the writers refuse to suffer the atrocities of an evil regime. These adolescents have seen how the power of words slowly permeates the soul until each Afghan can write of the fragrance of pomegranates, the colorful flames in a graveyard, the hope after self-immolation, a daughter's small lips mumbling for love.

In this last year, I have begun to connect the two marginalized groups through an exchange of poetry. My hope and the hope of their iO sponsoring teachers is that by erasing the geographical boundaries between Detroit and Kabul, the students will come to see that we are one and that out of our individual chaos comes the whole, a new reality springing from the power of the pure word. Or, as one Detroit sixth grade poet writes about how it feels to read an Afghan girl's poem: "I can feel the love coming from her poem in my veins. When I feel that love, the flow is really peaceful."

To feel such empathy for, and to reassure, people from another culture can only give self-worth and empowered status to the student poet. My students have written poems responding to individual writers and are beginning to receive feedback from an international audience. The exchanges are quite beautiful. As one of my Detroit students wrote to an Afghan woman, "I was welcomed. I was loved. I was brought into your world, as you were brought into mine." Their ELA and Social Studies teachers see the empathetic poetry their students are writing as an integral way to help them envision productive, successful future lives.

Their teachers are proud of the way learnings from this project spill over into other classroom work. One student recently used concepts from this exchange in his weekly vocabulary quiz. The teachers also say that this writing has given their students a chance

to realize their own rights. As young people who do have the freedom to attend school, who can speak their minds, who can challenge
cultural stereotypes, these Detroit adolescents feel privileged to be
able to offer support to their Afghan sisters. Thus, they become the
entitled, powerful advisors, those with access to education. As one
seventh grade student writes in response to an Afghan girl's essay
about being tyrannized by the Taliban:

> I wish you the power
> to cry very loudly
> so I can hear you
> from across the
> world
> I wish you to have the
> life I am living
> to save your people
> I wish I could take back
> centuries of your
> crying
> I wish you
> would pursue happiness
> and feel my
> empathy.

GLEYN ADAMS

As well as responding to the women in poems of their own, the
Detroit students, many of whom live amidst poverty and violence,
have talked and written about the volunteer work they plan to do
in the future with the persecuted and underserved. In addition to
a beautiful sense of empathy, their writing displays a grasp of the
power of silence as a precursor to self-evaluation. They seem to have
developed a unique capacity to feel the intense pain of their global
counterparts and to talk about it. In one of the many conferences I
conducted with my students about the Afghan poems they had read,
a sixth grade boy told me, "I love these poems even though they hurt
my soul. I love the writer so much, the powerful words I love."

My soul resounds with the beauty of the discoveries made in

the InsideOut classrooms and soars with the imagistic offerings of strength created each week. Perhaps, quite soon, these students from opposite ends of the globe will be writing poetry together and reading it to a more equitable, peaceful world. As for now, when one Afghan girl writes of the pain of being born a girl in a country where she is not worthy to speak, a twelve-year-old boy from the east side of Detroit writes to her with hope and love:

> I wish you the happiest days and nights in the corner of your room.
> I wish I could hear you cry tears of joy and see you read as much as you want.
> I wish you could find a better place just for you.
> I wish I had a mind wipe and could make you forget the bad things that happened to you.
> I wish we could write a poem together and read it to the world.
> JALEN SINGLETON

# The Adolescent Heart

*Julia Putnam*

I became a teacher because I wanted to marry my love of literature and my love of conversation. I love to talk with young people, in particular. I am fascinated by identity-formation in adolescents. Writing poems at this time in life is tricky. Teenagers are all so vulnerable and confused about all the movement in the world around them and their inner lives and physical appearance that poems often serve as a conduit of emotions. They are often just glorified diary entries. And for anyone who has ever kept a diary, you know that we both *want* people to read our thoughts and feelings and are simultaneously mortified by the mere idea of anyone being privy to them.

It was my job as an InsideOut writer-in-residence to help the students see poetry as not just diary entries but also art, a craft, a chance to mold words into shapes as if they were clay. This was not my strength.

I did not consider myself a poet. I was a student of poetry, but I was completely intimidated by people with the confidence to claim the title. My colleagues at InsideOut were *real* poets. I was the roadie hanging out with the band; I was the batgirl in the major leagues. While I was reading book after book of poetry, they were submitting their own poems to journals and selling their chapbooks at local readings. They were trying out different poetic forms for themselves and teaching them to students—using foreign words I had not even learned in school, words like sestinas and cinquains.

I had to rely on what I did know: the earnestness of the adolescent heart. Even at twenty-six, I could remember so viscerally my sixteen-year-old self. When I was sixteen, I was an obedient, eager-to-please dreamer with questions about why the world worked the way it did. Most of my questions were about Detroit and why people talked about it with the wistful tone of the past tense. I wondered what this hopelessness meant for my own future in this place.

My questions were answered by a couple named James and Grace Lee Boggs. James and Grace Lee are two influential and well-respected community activists in Detroit. They are revolutionary thinkers who founded a volunteer youth program in 1992. Modeled after Freedom Summer that occurred during the Civil Rights Movement, Detroit Summer was designed to respirit, rebuild, and redefine Detroit from the ground up. In asking me to make a difference in my community, I felt hope that the bleak future people predicted for Detroit did not have to come to pass, and, finally, I felt the best parts of myself were being called upon to make a contribution to a higher purpose. My desire to make a real difference in the world would not be wasted in service to the stagnant requirements of high school—good grades and compliance.

Detroit Summer taught me many things, one of the most useful being that I loved taking part in meaningful conversation. Even today, at 99, Grace does not suffer idle chatter well. If you are with her, you are going to be asked important questions about the state of the world and I had decided that I would be the kind of person who would try to have an answer. And I knew she would listen.

This tendency of the adults in Detroit Summer to take young people seriously, to believe that they had an important contribution to make to the conversation, shaped the way I approached my role as an InsideOut writer. I could not be the best poet; but I could listen to what young people had to say about their lives.

As I look back at the poems that were written on my watch, very few of them are as artfully crafted as I would like. I told myself then that it was because I was a bad poet myself, that I didn't have the skill to do better or teach better. I realize now that this is not all true. What I know now is that what was important to me was to do as Jimmy and Grace did: to take their voices seriously.

What I was good at was standing in front of young people and sensing their simultaneous desire and fear: they wanted to express themselves yet they were afraid that they were singularly inadequate and foolish. Oh, how I knew how they felt! And so I modeled vulnerability. I was able to deflect skepticism by enthusiastically reading aloud my favorite poems, no matter how silly I looked or sounded. I remember one student demanding, with a recalcitrant *Oh, yeah?* in her eyes: "*Poetry*? Can you say one right now? By heart?"

And so I recited "Nothing Gold Can Stay" by Robert Frost—the poem I memorized when I was twelve because I read it in the young adult novel *The Outsiders* by S. E. Hinton, and it spoke to my fear that no matter how happy I was at any given moment, it would go away. I was always so concerned with the fleeting nature of joy. I told the kids that I carried that book in my back pocket throughout 7th grade because I couldn't bear being too far away from my favorite characters. I told them how, when I finished the book, I was so overcome with emotion that I started sobbing. My mother walked in to see what was going on. "What is wrong with you?" she said. "Johnnycakes died!" I wailed. "Oh girl," my mother smacked. "I thought something was wrong with you!" And she closed the door, going back to her exhausting single-mother tasks that could not be interrupted by the dramatic fancies of a preteen. Inevitably, kids would smile appreciatively at that story. They knew well the dismissal of wary and harried adults.

One brilliant aspect of InsideOut is having the classroom teachers participate in the writing process with the students. Not all teachers participated, but mine often did—at least in the writing part. It was always harder to get teachers to share. I will never forget David Wayntraub, a middle-aged Jewish man with a yarmulke, in a classroom populated solely by Black students, volunteering to share the poem he had written in class. It was about his son and the students were able to ask questions about his home life. This act of vulnerability on Mr. Wayntraub's part built trust with his students that I saw resonate for the rest of the year. He did it only once and never again, but it didn't matter. The students had seen behind the wall.

And so they shared as well. Intense declarations of love for their parents and siblings, grave stories of loss and loneliness. The subject matter revealed such a weight in children's lives and a striking contrast between their developmental immaturity and the sobering emotional responsibilities they carried. There were poems about insecurity, being "too black," friends who'd been killed in hit-and-run accidents, homes that got raided by police officers while at dance practice, talks of masks that they put on to hide their true selves.

Sometimes, the students would present a first draft of a poem and wonder why I would ever suggest another. I remember feeling conflicted many times about the students who felt proud for even putting words to the page. Hadn't they bared their souls for the entire world to see and wasn't that soul beautiful, as is? *You want me to do more?* They were even more self-congratulatory when they would read their pieces aloud. I found it hard to challenge this and only got better in time through the mentorship I received from my colleagues at InsideOut. I learned which poems to use as model texts for revision and how to pace my sessions with the students so that that there was time in the school year to revise in deliberate, rather than frantic, ways.

Most often, after we'd talk about how the power of language often comes forth only after we play with it, and I would rave about a particular line in a particular poem—either for its specific detail or a surprising metaphor—I would be able to get students to tweak their initial revelations and raw pain into lines like these:

"I was pouring blue Kool-Aid into a glass cup / Decorated with lemons."

"In my dream, I wake up to hear myself scream / like an opera lady doing her solo part."

"I am a dictionary, full of meaning."

"I am a fireplace filled with lots of sparks that light people's faces."

Reading the drafts often left me sad about the emotions of children that often went unaddressed in the classroom. I wanted more time with students and longed for a classroom of my own. I left InsideOut to become a full-time classroom teacher. Six years ago, I began developing a school with other educators who were also inspired by Jimmy and Grace, particularly their idea about community-building as a tool for learning. The mission of the James and Grace Lee Boggs School is to nurture creative, critical thinkers who contribute to the well-being of their communities. The founders believe that we must prepare students to live in a future they are given tools to help create, in addition to preparing them to exist in a present reality that is rapidly changing. We must teach our children to shape the world in the same way I once asked them to shape words.

We just finished the first year of the James and Grace Lee Boggs School, and it is clearly the poem I was meant to write. I am so proud to have had InsideOut as part of this path.

# Indelible Moments

*John Rybicki*

A few years ago, teaching at a last-chance high school in Detroit, I spread my arms with my palms facing upward like a priest's. I asked my students, "What if you could amass in one hand all the bounty and joy, all the sweet things you've experienced wearing this skin? How much would this palm hold?" Then I swung my eyes to the other hand. "What if you heaped in this hand all the hard and harrowing things, the earthquake weather of the human heart? Which palm would hold more?"

I asked for a show of hands. The palm with sorrow or duress in it won the vote by a landslide.

Next, I folded one hand over the other so both extremes could meet and meld. I read to them a prose poem about the night my dad came home drunk and we bare-knuckle boxed in the kitchen—a night wherein there was august love woven into a psychically and physically violent event.

Gordon Lish writes, "Your grief is your fortune as a writer." My beloved wife once told me, through the ache in her brown eyes, "At least you got some powerful poems from my cancer." Am I to give thanks for human suffering when out of it springs my most potent song?

I ask students to make a list of three core moments in their lives they associate with each hand, moments that if they lived to be ten-thousand years old those memories will never wash away. The best writing, as Faulkner aptly put it, is summoned from "the problems of the human heart in conflict with itself which alone can make good writing because only that is worth writing about, worth the agony and the sweat." You simply cannot write a potent poem with a block of ice in your chest. It involves emotional and imaginative jeopardy. When poets dip their pens, for example, into the palm that holds sublime joy, they draw back that pen with starlight dripping from it.

I want them impassioned, ticking in their own skin before I release them to the page. I lead them there by telling stories from my own childhood.

I'm sleeping on a tightrope the night, as a little boy, I first hear my father cry through the papery wall. Some dark angel is reaching into his chest and tearing up by the roots those discordant cries. I hear this never-before thing. I catch his locomotive gasps and cries in the mitt of my boy spirit.

At that very moment my elbow slips and thunks against the wall. My father starts grabbing those sobs and stuffing them by the fistful back in his chest until there's almost no sound in the world. My bedroom window purses its lips and exhales all the wind in the world.

One one-thousand, two one-thousand, three. My father knuckle-knocks one knock back. I light a bright boy-smile in the dark. I knock back twice. He laughs and knocks back with three hits. I go four. He goes five. Now he's gusting great bursts of laughter as he beats his fists in a drum roll against the wall. I'm beating mine in time. My mom's arms rise like flames from a burn barrel to swaddle around this man and drag him back down to bed.

What are you doing? What on earth are you doing?

I'm loving my boy. I'm loving my boy.

The bulk of what I experienced that year as a boy has been muted into memory. That night will never wash away. Your job as a wordsmith, I tell students, is to transport us back in time, to paint vividly with language so that a piece of paper becomes a kind of live, breathing movie screen in your reader's hand. You can, in fact, erase the world around them to where you steep them in the world you are re-creating with language. Remember, you have a movie reel in your brain with striking details from your core life experiences, but we were not there. Slow time. Be a keen observer. Dip your paintbrush into an array of colors.

Here's one about the time I first swore as a boy, and my father chased me through the house.

We're in the breakfast nook eating dinner, all six of us Rybickis pinched in with my father at the head of the table in the get-away

zone. Dark thunder clappers mound up in his face. They start beating their fists against the table so the silverware chimes and jumps
and when it lands our plates are all in a wobble. A couple of chicken
legs jump ship off my brother Benny's plate. The peas spill over-
board, too. Little brother Michael lunges back and gets bug-smashed
against the wall. Then Dad backhands a gallon jug of milk and sends
it chugging milk into my mother's lap.

Snap.

Little red Irish boy rage.

My mouth turns bullhorn as I unleash every swear word I ever
heard fly from my father's mouth. "Fuck this shit. Fuck all this shit."
Wet bullets jump out of my eyes and they don't even touch my
cheeks. I rocket up on his left and duck under his swoop of arms so
he's hugging only air. I cut past him into daylight sending a second
volley of cuss back over my shoulder. "Cocksucking muthafucker."

My words wallop him at first. There's a shock in his face like an
electric snow is falling inside him. Then the pilot light oomphs back
on and with it that blowtorch of rage hitting against every inch of
his skin.

He's bucking out of his chair, flying back with my brother Benny
and sister Lisa each diving for one of his legs. Mom crashes into him
like a feathery linebacker trying to bring him down. He's shucking
them off like flies. I bang up the spiral staircase past a wall-hung
Christ, hook right down the hall with him thumping on my tail. Cut
left into my bedroom then right as I stride and leap onto the radia-
tor doing a face-first Superman dive out the window.

I ball up and cat tumble onto the porch's metal skin, come out
of the tuck with the momentum carrying me into the ropes. Our
wooden railing rocks some but braces my back. Pops ruptures
through Lisa's bedroom door—her room's next to ours. Her screen
door slaps back against the bricks with Pops in a bull rush towards
me. I leap the railing to the gutter, and it springs up and down like
a diving board.

He's on me. I have one fast choice: face the beast or leap. I release
and lunge back into space, feel myself riding the air away from him.
Only my father snaps a left jab and catches a fistful of my white
T-shirt even as I'm falling. I bob up and down under his fist like a

Christmas ornament, two or three bobs, and then the shirt shreds up all around me. He's left holding nothing but my shirt.

Students will begin to leap in with stories of their own. Invariably, they will, in the telling, skim over the events without the musculature of vivid imagery. I ask questions that will help illuminate a piece. I invite students to close their eyes while they listen to another student telling their tale.

Recently, at Martin Luther King, Jr. High School, a boy volunteered to tell a brave and luminous, haunting tale from his life. What transpired was so emotionally charged, this boy altered the very molecules in the room. It was only the third time in decades of teaching that something so sacred happened that I wanted to end the class. Or rather, I wanted to end class, find the nearest church, and fall down on my knees in prayer. This slender, wise, brave young man named Amon Adjuman socked everyone in that classroom with a spiritual fist.

## Abijan
*For my grandmother*

I lived with my grandma in Ivory Coast, Africa, until I was eight. She had arthritis so bad that when she stood up it was like she was bleeding through her knees. She'd send us out in the morning to tend the garden, or to pick lettuce, tomatoes, squash, and corn. We were sharecroppers. That garden was our life. One time wild dogs destroyed our crops. We had nothing to eat, nothing to trade with, no seeds to replant.

My grandma and her mother grew that garden. It had been in our family a long time. In our village we don't believe a place is haunted; we believe the spirits of our ancestors watch over us. When we worry or suffer, they eat our problems. The third day after the dogs had destroyed everything, I went to the garden. An enormous squash had bloomed out of nowhere.

On what was our Halloween, the people in the village would walk through the graveyard to pray and be with our ancestors. One time there was a pack of those dogs there. Grandma called them demon dogs because they would bite people who had done something wrong. That evening the dogs were attacking certain people when the spirits of our ancestors rose up and the dogs got silent. The spirits pushed the dogs back to where they had been standing.

When I was little, I'd gather water for the garden from a nearby stream. I would do some weeding. I'd also get the mud and clay and sand to help build the clay pots we sold. In the evening my grandmother would cook and we'd tell stories. She spoke once of a mouse with a brotherly disposition. It was close to a crow, so it would not tell the cats where the crow did its hiding. One day the crow told the cats where to find the mouse, and the cats ripped the mouse to shreds.

Sometimes my uncle came from the city to visit. He was a self-taught carpenter. We cut down a giant tree in front of our house, and he made a cane with four legs out of one of the branches. One morning Grandma said, "Forget everything else. I want to go to my garden." She wanted to give the garden her own love. It normally took fifteen minutes to get to the garden. It took us an hour with Grandma that day. She'd stop at times and lean against a tree. It looked like she had tears in her eyes. I'd go to her, but she'd say, "No, I'm OK."

The journey passed in stages. We'd go through tall grasses and milkweed at first. Then there was a bare patch with broken trees and logs. After that we passed through the muddy patch where I got our clay. The mud would get hard from the sunshine. Grandma was happy. She had given me red dirt to plant with the squash and it made the flowers on those plants turn red. It made her cry it was so beautiful. We also had this circle garden about as big as a round table for four. Grandma planted a tulip in the center of it, but it would never grow. It dried up and died every year. That day the tulip was in full bloom!

We tended the garden for an hour or more. Then I heard cries, screams. I thought it was this crazy woman in our village. It got louder and louder. My grandma had a question mark on her face. I didn't have glasses then, but I thought I saw someone through the milkweed. Suddenly a man jumped out with a hand gun, spear, and machete. It looked like he was running towards me. My grandma was three feet away. I was lunging towards her. The man ran and threw the spear. It hit my grandmother in the center of her chest. He had this look in his eyes like he wanted to kill me, but I guess a war chief cried out and he ran back.

My grandma had enough time to talk to me before she died, but I don't think I can tell you what she said.

Our hearts hit the floor and they did not get up. An unspeakable power filled that room. You could take a coffee cup and scoop a kind of fire right out of the air.

This ninth grade seer, in his initial telling, told a vivid tale but skimmed over so many important details. When we sat down to revise I urged him to slow time and be a keen observer, paint with language in such a way that you baptize us in the landscape of your memory. I asked questions about the grandma, the landscape around their village. Lush sentences tumbled off this boy's tongue. He erased the school around me. I was across the ocean hovering in the air near their lives and witnessing it all.

The following poem was written by a high school student who, for weeks, swore to me she couldn't write a poem.

### This Is What I Want You to See
My grandfather's in his hospital bed
taking his last breaths and everyone is crying.
Our eyes are all red and puffy.
Tears roll down all our faces.
My mom is holding his hand.
My grandmother is in the hospital bed
lying beside him. How can I get through this?
I wanted it to be a dream so badly,
but when I heard the *dinnnnnng*
of the machine and saw the white line
I knew it was real. A sudden memory crept
across my face. My grandfather would say
*bang bang bang* at the dinner table; *bang bang bang*

when he watched tv; *bang bang bang*
when we walked to the store.
Can you see what I see now?
Is your heart a boat made of glass
shattered along the shore?

KIARA JOHNSON

Her sorrowful prayer is, as Rudyard Kipling once wrote, ". . . all the worlds and mine." She illuminates not only the scene but a revealing part of her grandfather's nature. And her luminous and heartfelt ending baptizes the rest of the poem in flame. The emotional payoff is tremendous.

I hit them with Huckleberry Finn adventures I had as a boy. They tell stories born out of adventures from their childhood, family stories, illness or love or death. The activity takes them to the soul of who they are. I remind them that their stories and poems fortify a culture and sometimes elevate the human spirit to where they remind their readers, as in this poem, that we are all members of one human family.

# What Poetry Has to Do with Any of It

*Anna Clark*

Three years into my writing residencies in Detroit high schools, there are patterns.

I arrive in the mornings with my shoulders tilted into spine-bending bags brimming with folders. My coffee spills onto the cuff of my coat. Whether I'm at the high school that is old and over-heated, or the school that is gleaming new, there is a nod-and-smile with the security guards as I pass through a bleeping metal detector.

There are patterns.

But what I am unable to do is hook into any single narrative about what urban public high schools under emergency management are like, or what Teenagers These Days are like, or what poetry has to do with any of it.

I spend the school year wondering about how my Hmong students at Osborn High School come from a culture without a written language. I wonder how to talk about metaphor with the deaf students at the Detroit School of Arts, who speak in signs already. I wonder why the students are never so rapt as when I tell them stories about Harry Houdini.

I'm rapt by the intensity of it all. These teenagers are in the time of life when you simply haven't lived long enough to see yourself change: you really believe you'll never love again because you've never known yourself to love again. I'd almost forgotten the feeling.

I want to tell you all their stories, but really, they can tell their own stories.

There is the ninth grade girl with dimples who was startled by how much her poem about her grandmother dying influenced us when she read it aloud: her teacher cried. I'm fond of the short girl with glasses, a sophomore, who is loud, doesn't like to write, and walks in and out of the room all during class, but who once paged through a book of Ai's poems and liked them. There is the tall girl who dramatically wails, "I don't know what to *write*! Tell me what to *write*!" and then writes. One boy, an eleventh grader who twice beat me at chess, is quiet and presses his pencil so deep into his paper it's as if he is cutting it. Another boy (tenth grade) moves to a desk in the corner of the room, away from us all, and bows his head in concentration as he makes letters that are really hard for him to make.

At one of my first InsideOut high schools, we spent the last month of the school year hosting a Wednesday afternoon open mic. There was a rousing set of regulars in the auditorium or the library, wherever we could find a place to gather each week, but attendance could sometimes be patchy—at least among the students in my three poetry classes. But on our last Wednesday showcase, four boys from my ninth grade class showed up. One of the boys blasted down the auditorium aisle and signed up to perform. I'll call him Cyrus.

Here's the thing about Cyrus: he is fourteen, but it looks as if he is nine. He is approached as if he were a toy. The other boys like to pick him up and pass him around. They tilt him over their shoulders and shake him.

Cyrus doesn't shirk. He'll flail his limbs and loudly (if ineffectively) yell for the boys to leave him alone. He is nervy, spastic, utterly off-the-wall with energy: you can see the nine-year-old in him, just under the surface. He loves comics and adores the *Avengers* movie. He'll volunteer to read aloud just about any poem I bring in, before I ask, and whether or not anyone is listening. He fidgets and is noisy and likes to say something—often nonsense—in any gap of quiet he finds. Cyrus is also immensely smart: just very sharp, particularly with language, and he has a wealth of knowledge pocketed inside him that comes out abruptly, in the form of trivia or condescending corrections to someone else's supposed lapse: "They're not chitlins; they're chitterlings!"

Most of what Cyrus writes is goofy stuff. It's lines he'll run off in seconds and play for maximum laughs. He will not revise a single thing, no matter what I say or do. His favorite piece is a rap about bacon. For months, he keeps sneaking up behind me while I'm talking to other students, and he'll launch in, rhyming "bacon" with "taken," and "hot" with "a lot."

Cyrus, I say. Take a breath.

I love that he is playful with his words. But I suspect that Cyrus is using humor to deflect: it's his comic-book hero's shield. For a person who has more than his share of vulnerabilities in a very tough school, silliness is his safest space.

When Cyrus signed up for the open mic, I was sure he was going to do his bacon rap. His turn comes up, he climbs up on that stage before about 40 kids, and, oh look . . .

Cyrus has memorized his poem. It is called "How to be a Man." I've never heard or read it before. He performs it anxiously, his hands in his pockets, fidgeting, and he stops once when he stumbles: "I'm nervous." But Cyrus speaks loudly, in large bursting exhales. He has conviction before rows of people who are almost universally older and larger than him. One senior is carrying around a shot put, as part of his athletic training. Another student, a good-looking junior, has two composition books full of poems on his knee; his dominating presence at the open mics never fails to impress the ladies.

In front of them all, Cyrus unleashes a litany of images, in a poem pearled with rhetorical questions. It is good! A thoughtful articulation of what we load on to the idea of "manhood." But here's the thing that moves me most: Cyrus means it.

It's brave enough to get up there for the first time and perform your own work. It's quite another thing to risk meaning what you say.

# Dangerous Acts

*Nandi Comer*

*For Dwoyne Joiner and all the risk takers*

**Sounds**
On the street of Joy Road, dope boys pushing work and the
    police
are scheming. At night you hear the pistol go boom and the
    people
start screaming. It's people across the street getting thrown out
    and
the house on the corner burning up.

You hear the sound *whea whea* on the big red truck. It's the girls
fighting on the corner, while their moms are looking out the
    door,
ashamed of their daughters. In the winter you hear the Nike
    boots
crunch in the snow.

You hear the Expedition go *boom boom* as it goes. There are
many sounds as you enter the hood of Joy Road.

BRITTNEY BLACK

I helped Brittney Black write this poem while I was teaching at Frank
Cody High School. I think about this poem a lot because its writer
gained a lot of popularity during my time teaching there. Brittney
had memorized it and many of her classmates liked to hear her recite it repeatedly. When I read this poem the images depicting the
neighborhood surrounding Cody feel somewhat celebratory while
at the same time dangerous. Like my students I grew up in the Cody
neighborhood, so I'm sure I also return to Brittney's poem because
it is representative of a neighborhood that I am familiar with. But

Brittney's poem is not the poem I always return to when I think of my time at Cody.

Actually, I can't publish the poem I most remember. It's a lot like the poem above and does some of things the above poem does in that it also has violent imagery and tension. Both poems take risks, using language to depict haunting experiences. I chose the poem above for its approximation to the missing poem, but the missing poem is riskier than the one above.

The missing poem—let's call it "Loss"—was composed during a writing activity where I asked students to write about an unforgettable event or moment in their lives. After reading Lucille Clifton's poem "The 1st" and discussing Clifton's use of vivid imagery, I lead students through an exercise asking them to close their eyes and return to the place of their memory. Behind closed eyelids students recreated sensory details they associated with those moments. Then I asked students to take to the page, reminding them to include all the sensory details they had just re-created in their imaginations. Once students felt they had something to share, they volunteered to read aloud. Some of them had memories about their favorite birthday or the time they got a new pair of sneakers, but then there was a student who wrote about losing his mother.

The student, I'll call him "David," described a graphic scene where his mother was murdered by another family member. David expressed the pain he felt losing his mother to violence. He also addressed the poem to his mother's assassin, which gave it a complicated voice speaking out directly to the person that had harmed him. David seemed relieved after he finished reading his poem. He seemed as if he had finally allowed himself to directly challenge his mother's death. The rest of us didn't know what to say. Some of us sat in awkward silence.

Some writers describe their engagement with youth who have lost loved ones to violence as a process of healing, but I am resistant towards taking on that role. It seems inappropriate for me to claim to *heal* my students of their traumas. Sure, it helps the students to talk, but I don't think of the writing they create with me as an ointment to rub over a wound until it crusts into a scab, eventually becoming a barely noticeable mark. The writing in "Loss" had a very different purpose. This was David's way of lifting up his sleeve and demanding that the community look at his scar. Dealing with his mother's death meant naming it. It meant calling out the names of his abusers. That kind of poem is not only hard to write, it's also the hardest kind of poem to hear from one of your students. David was asking us to see him whole. Other students wrote poems that day about falling in love with football, overcoming bullies, and keeping their heads in the books. Those poems can be beautiful, but they are oftentimes safe. David's poem entered the dangerous business of risk taking. This opportunity to address his pain and loss could also put him in danger.

Later I typed David's poem to include it in the school's anthology, but when the time came to choose which poems would be published, it was decided that for his protection the poem could not be preserved as written. He would have to remove all names and incriminating details associated with the loss of his mother in order for it to be included in the book. David and I worked on the poem, but out of frustration maybe, or impatience, he decided to pull the poem and no version exists for the public to read. That poem in its printed form is lost. Gone.

Though that poem is erased from the memory of Cody I think about it often. It took a risk that not many youth are willing to take. Poems like "Loss" say, *Look at what you have done. Look at what we are becoming. Look at our scars.*

Sometimes teachers will say that the poems students write about violence are not well crafted, or that they don't resonate, but I think these kinds of poems make us in the adult world uncomfortable. These are the kinds of poems that place in front of us some stark truths. Students need to be able to write poems that make us uncomfortable because, in truth, they are calling us out. Their writing asks us to see them and their world as it really is and not some edited smoothed-out version. David and writers like him remind us that there are young people who are losing parts of themselves.

David's poem seemed essential to his mourning process. David's poem took a definite risk. I am not sure I have ever taken such risks in my own writing. I still worry for his safety. I worry about the people around him. I remember my experiences with David and his poem. I celebrate him. I say, "I hear you."

# Going Home

*Gloria Nixon-John*

My first home was a rented upper flat on Detroit's Heidelberg Street. Once my parents were able they bought a five-room, post-WWII bungalow on Detroit's East Side. Many of the memories I have of my early years in Detroit are framed in the view I had from the attic window of that home. As a pre-teen that attic was my quiet place. I saw the ordinary from that window, wash billowing on the neighbor's clothesline, heard the sensual sounds of Della Reese floating up from the newlyweds' window below. I saw mysterious things, too—a long, finned sedan pulling into a vacant field, two silhouettes on the front seat moving together to become one large shadowy amalgamation. Later, in college, the Modernists (I am giving away my age away here) gave me permission to focus my writing on home, or to at least to use home as a starting point. I refer here to Sherwood Anderson's short story cycle, *Winesburg Ohio*, and Thomas Wolfe's *Look Homeward Angel*. Even when Virginia Woolf urged me to find a room of my own I imagined—still imagine—that room on the periphery of what I identify both literally and figuratively as home. So, in 2001, when I was invited to work with children as a writer-in-residence for InsideOut at Coffey Middle School, I had the notion that I was going home. I was in fact going home to the city of my birth. It seemed quite natural, a synchronicity of sorts, for me to approach my students with this notion of home, to start them off writing their experiences of home or hometown. I also wanted to share what I knew about craft, about revision, but the unexpected often happens in the classroom, and plans and preconceived notions often fall away before the more valuable lessons are learned.

To get the seventh grade students started I read a piece of narrative poetry that I had written about the attic of my childhood home and the view from that attic window:

The attic was all bare bones,
life stripped down to the bones,
the inside of the whale.
Raindrops hit the roof
in a jazzy rhythm,
muffled words filtered
up from the world below.
In the shadowy corner
a triage of dolls missing limbs
teddy bears worn thin.
Bright squares and rectangles
swelled and ebbed
on clotheslines below . . .

When I glanced up from my reading some of the students had those deep furrows between their eyes that told me I was sharing something confusing, or worse yet, boring. Similar approaches had worked before, why not now? Still, I plowed on—and those forehead furrows got deeper. Next, I gave the students an exercise in which I had them look out of a window in the place they called home, asked them to describe using all of their senses, to vary their perspective to describe things close at hand as well as those in the distance. The writing that a couple of the students offered to share as a result of that exercise was more static than I had expected. Had I thrown them off with my example? After all, my childhood experiences are ancient history. So, I did that little mental tap dance that teachers do when an activity isn't working as expected. I moved outward in my thinking, and I asked the students to go to a door in that place called home and to move out from there, to step out of the door and make some sense of what they were seeing, hearing, smelling.

"OK, but where are we going? Out the door I mean, where we going?" a tall boy in the back of the class asked, and the laughter spread, became a crescendo of incredulity.

Don't lose your cool. Smile, I told myself. "Anywhere you want to go," I said. I was starting to sweat. Was I failing? Was I out of my element? Not cool enough for these savvy, urban children? But,

Joy To The World, in a few short minutes they were writing. Twenty minutes later, when I asked them to stop writing so they could share what they had written, a half dozen arms flew up, stretched so that their open hands resembled a field of flowers turning toward the light. But it wasn't flowers and light that Steven Logan shared.

> When I walk out of my door in the morning I hear the police chasing off another criminal. The front lawn is glistening from the dew and the sun is shining down. I can smell something wonderful, like pancakes, sausages, and eggs from the kitchen, but soon I will see pushers on the street waiting for addicts to come through. When all I can do is get ready for school, and as I hear my baby sister go Wha Wha Wha, I know I'm gonna have to survive to see better things.

Many of the other students shared pieces that provided a similarly stark picture of the neighborhood around Coffey Middle School. This was not the Detroit neighborhood of my youth in the old neighborhood; it was rare to hear a police siren and if there were pushers and addicts in the neighborhood of my youth, they were hidden. Once I got past the pushers and addicts that Steven mentioned in his piece, I saw his hope, his resilience. He does all he can really do, he says. He gets ready for school, and he focuses on his determination to see better things. Maybe the sound of his little sister reminds him that there must be a better future.

Next, Tyrone read a paragraph in which he described trees rolling by, the black land beneath his passage there. He said that when he passed street signs, he wondered what the next sign would be until "a cloud of beauty" passed over him and he saw that cloud as rescue, as relief. He said he had, and could finally ask, question after question, questions that came pouring out "like water from a waterfall . . ." He then quoted his mother who answered his most important question, "I don't know why things just happen, but they do," she told him. He ended his piece with the words, "A moment of silence please."

OK, I was starting to get the idea that the students were not just searching for and finding the beauty around them; they were also finding hope, and were able to find that hope by transcending their environment. While Tyrone's piece is kind of cryptic (I could see lines of poetry in his prose), by the end of the piece we get the sense that something tragic has happened but that Tyrone has made something beautiful out of the tragedy.

As I continued to work with the children at Coffey Middle School, I started to view my role differently. I was there to give the students the time and freedom to write what they needed to write, independent of my notion of good craft. Teaching about craft could wait. It would come in due time. First they had to think, feel, write. But this revelation didn't mean that my ignorance, my naiveté, had lifted completely. I remember having still another awakening while working with a clear-eyed girl named Shirley who I met up with in the school library. She sat down in a chair across from me to apologize, told me that she had trouble writing about home because she never had a home, not a real home in the way that most of us know home. She confided that she had gone from foster home to foster home because her mother was an addict and her father was in prison. She told me that school was the closest place to home that she had. As Shirley stood to leave she handed me the poem below.

**Shirley Love**
Love is supposed to be real
It's supposed to stand through whatever
but I guess that doesn't apply to me
I've been hurt
All because you want to act crazy
My heart was scared
Because of your pleasure
But I learned to live with this type of love
I gave it a name
"Shirley Love"

SHIRLEY BOLDEN

Once I recognized what was happening, that many of the students were stepping beyond the notion I had of home (at least the home of my youth), I suggested that they imagine they are above their city in an airplane, leaving home. Here is what Shirley wrote:

### Into the Storm

Shirley Bolden buckled her seatbelt tight. She lifted the shade from the window and was amazed. She had never flown before. She indulged in the moment, wanted it to be a memory forever. Shirley was ready. She opened her gum and started chewing like her grandmother had told her to. She was never more excited but yet scared. She was headed for the orange-blue sky. As the plane elevated her heart beat faster. Pain shot through her ears leaving a striking pain she had never experienced before. Over the intercom came a song, "Never in a thousand years will you ever get this feeling." Shirley's ears stopped ringing and she sighed in relief. The plane was small and a storm was approaching. Once into the storm the wind pushed the plane from side to side. Silence fell over the passengers . . .

Shirley ended her piece as illustrated above, and I like to think that she left the ending open, up to the reader, for a reason. I think she wanted us to go where we had to go, to decide if the story would end in a tragedy, or in survival. And she gave herself that opening too.

Clearly the students at Coffey Middle School taught me a valuable lesson about teaching, about my preconceived notion of what those particular students, at this time and in this place, needed. They also reminded me that time changes everything, that it's true, we *can't* go home again. Despite the darkness in many of the pieces that the students shared (and don't I wish I could tell you that I discovered that the neighborhoods are safe, families intact, etc., but I won't sugarcoat what too many of Detroit's children experience), there was almost always an expression of hope and resilience therein as well. Many of the stories and poems expressed the writers' ability to make sense of their lives, to transcend the circumstances of their lives, to rise above. And, as is usually the case for the teacher who is willing to admit it, teaching changes the teacher as well. As a result of the honesty of those students, I knew that when I went back to write about my childhood in Detroit, I would face the darkness in those stories that I was avoiding. I would take the proverbial rose-colored glasses off to get to the reality, a reality that I had to come to terms with, a reality I was free to transcend, but I had to face that reality first. I was reminded that working on craft, the right word in the right place is important to the writing, but only after I reveal some truth. I was ready to face up to everything I saw not just from that attic window, but also what I experienced in the world below. When I returned to my writing, I didn't write about drug addicts and pushers, didn't write about hearing gunshots in the neighborhood. That was not my experience. But I did write about the overt discrimination of that time, discrimination based on skin color, ethnicity, and economic status. I didn't shy away from writing about the neighborhood pedophile, or the neighbor lady who worshipped Adolf Hitler. I also wrote about how fortunate I was to live in that modest bungalow with two loving parents and a protective older brother. In doing so, I rediscovered the Detroit of my youth but more importantly, like my students, faced the stark realities of those life experiences, and was then able to transcend and make meaning of it all.

## Sharing Voices, Acting Crazy

*Cindy Frenkel*

My first year as a writer-in-residence with InsideOut, I was assigned to Henry Ford Academy in Highland Park, a straight shot down Woodward Avenue from where I live. Before my residency began, we had an orientation where I met the poet Jamaal May. He offered advice that serves me still. He explained how insecure and vulnerable the children feel, "so when you teach, act crazy," he said. "Make it so that whatever they do that feels like they're taking a risk isn't nearly as outside-the-box as what you've done." Before my first day, I took a test drive to the school. Not fifteen minutes from my suburban home, the urban decay surrounded me, buildings increasingly desolate, windows boarded-up or covered with metal grates. There was palpable energy in graffiti, although most was codified gang scrawling, a reminder that the oversize writing and symbols—forms of street art—are an outlet. I saw wig shops, adult entertainment places, and fast-food joints: no grocery stores or drug stores anywhere. In five miles, the world changed.

I turned onto Pilgrim, the school's street, and after a few blocks, opposite a caved-in house, stood the school. I wasn't prepared for this. Around the block, I came across a burned-out, factory-size building. What did I get myself into? Then, immediately after, shame hit as I thought that children live and go to school here every day.

What was it like to work there? And work there I did for three happy years—until it became a charter school. The school, though considered nicer than most, had exposed pipes (that was asbestos, wasn't it?), and teachers handed children pieces of toilet paper en route to the bathroom. The principal, who hailed from Brooklyn, was pleased I had lived in New York, and she was frustrated by the school's lack of diversity; almost everyone in the school was African American. During my second year, I discovered that the children assumed I, too, was African American because my hair was curly. (I'm pale and blue-eyed, but no matter.) I took it as the ultimate compliment.

My first day, I began falling in love. The students were open-eyed and talkative. I was animated and a bit off-the-wall, asking questions while moving around the room. "What is poetry? Why does writing matter? Who are you? How can writing transform your life?"

I soon realized how easy it is to attach labels, including the label "failure of the system." The "failure," it turns out, is a function of at least three factors: children living in poverty in one of the most affluent countries on the planet, lack of parental support, and parents' lack of support—a complicated mix. Many of us living elsewhere remain numb in the face of such overwhelming odds and anesthetize our consciousness, so we do nothing. I don't know if it's possible to grasp the challenges the children face without seeing them up close. I have had only a small glimpse, and it has widened the lens through which I observe life. (We use metaphors a lot in the classroom!)

As I taught the fundamentals of poetry (what a stanza is and a couplet and an off-rhyme, etc.), I also introduced them to many poets' work. I was enraptured when they reflected on "How Do I Love Thee?" and "To thine own self be true." When they'd get overly rowdy, I'd pick up "the invisible phone," dive into a one-sided dialogue, and this would reengage them. Those were comical, impromptu conversations. "You want William to do what?" I'd ask incredulously. "But that's illegal! All right, I'll tell him . . ." I'd turn to William, "You're supposed to write about what it's like to drive a car!" I'd try out emerging characters that I'd have improvised for friends or performed during a poetry reading, always speaking in different accents. These became favored requests by the children. When asked to do so, I'd comply by questioning, "OK, you guys. British, Yiddish, or Southern? You choose!" Often a poem had to be recited all three ways. I hammed it up, commenting on the poem in character, and they adored it, hamming it up back. I became a Southern belle, replete with proper mannerisms. Whatever I did, I made it up on the spot, and it worked. "My, my, you kiiiids are actin' wiiiild. Calm down, darlin's!" or "Oy! Youz a beee-u-tiful groowp of childlen'! Ven I vas yourh h, vee didn't have no plumin'. In de' Olt Countree . . . Oy! Life is hart heeerh, but oy vey! Vee had troublse,

79

too! And dey vas bik ones!" It wired them up in the best way. Some-times I'd recite poems and add gestures, which they often wanted to learn. Talk about fun!

For two more years, I followed several fourth, fifth, and sixth graders, and I watched them gain insights while developing their voices. When iO sponsored the National Endowment for the Art's Big Read in Detroit, each student received a copy of Dickinson's poems. First, I explained that once there was a poet, Miss Emily. I described the time, her room, and her clothes. "Where do you think she lived?" I asked. Bobby, a delightful sixth grader with caramel-colored eyes, eagerly raised his hand, tilting his head. I nodded, and he asked, "In the hood?" (I couldn't resist writing a poem entitled, "Emily D. in the Hood.") I watched a husky, impatient fifth grader light up, waving his hand in the air, announcing, "This is my favorite Emily poem!" and then, moments later, blurt out, "No, this is!"

Some things can't be rushed; they develop slowly and deliberate-ly—the rapport one has with kids is such a thing. Once they knew me well enough, I heard their heartbreaking realities. When one student was more withdrawn than usual, I questioned her, and she casually explained her cousin was getting out of prison that day. "He was playing Russian roulette with his brother . . ."

Writing worked its cathartic powers. They hungered to put their voices to paper. (I know its draw firsthand; it is my balm in troubled times, my trumpet in happy ones.) When I taught Bobby, word was out among teachers that he and his friends formed a gang. I walked up to him with paper and pen in hand. "I heard you've formed a gang," I admonished him. "What's its name?" He looked up, stating, "School Boys." I wrote it down. "Who's in the gang?" I demanded. He politely listed names. I wrote them down, aware of his tender com-pliance. I pointed my finger at him, "You don't want to be in a gang! I want better for you. Do you hear me?" He nodded. I felt honored by his trust, but I also knew full well that by the eighth grade, it was unlikely he would be so open.

I'd like to say that these things were anomalies, but that's not ac-curate. When the fifth grade teacher changed classrooms in mid-day to teach across the hall, she locked her classroom door. Someone pried open that door with a crowbar and stole her purse.

The violence, poverty, and despair were more than I could have imagined, yet some children have indomitable spirits. Their buoyancy helped me. It was as if I were working with angels, spirits housed in small, beautiful bodies. They wrote about the joys of family life, loving parents, pets, siblings, grandparents, and they wrote of broken homes and broken-down neighborhoods. When they read their poems, their self-esteem seemed to rise; they stood up straighter, and they spoke loudly and with pride.

They understood Mies van der Rohe's line, "God is in the details." One time, after we'd finished going over metaphors and similes, a shy, quiet boy wrote:

**The Pencil**
This pencil in my hand
is rough. Like an old table,

orange like a tiger.
Short eraser, like a light switch.

Hard as a desk.
Skinny as a line.

                              JOHN CRAFT

That light switch/eraser image is one I can't forget. Another poem is by a sprightly fourth grader who improvised characters with me and held his own as if we were contemporaries (I swear our unlikely pairing was so strong that we could be on stage together). His name is Robert Porter-McDowell. We made up stories about a mouse in his "office" (because of the computer mouse) and when we entered different places via the computer's keys, we had to press "enter" to go to the oddest stops. I'd call out, "Rooooooooooooooo-bert!" and he'd jump up, match my movement, then add his own zingy twist.

We couldn't have been much wittier or more inane, but when he got down to writing about sad things, he entered a whole other world. I admire this poem for its heartbreaking grace and honesty in a story aptly told:

*Cindy Frenkel*

**Worst Days of My Life**
On December 3, 2010,
My cousin Ray Ray
Got shot ten times at a store.
Somebody shot him for no reason.
The first time they shot five times,
Then he got up and started running.
He got shot five more times.
Then he died.
I was devastated on that day.

On November 23, 2010, at 11:45,
My pastor died.
Cause he had cancer.
We went to his funeral.
I was scared.
Everyone was crying, screaming
And when my sister Latrice
And my cousin Martez and I
Went up there and saw him
I almost dropped a tear on his face.
I miss him.

ROBERT PORTER-MCDOWELL

That poem was published in their last anthology, and when I came to school bearing those books—one for every author!—I felt like Santa. The book was the tangible thing, yet what I like to think I left the children with was the value of articulating their ideas, and the gift of reading, a way to journey without leaving home, their ticket between the covers of a book.

What I didn't know was how much the children would affect me. At year's end, Bobby approached me and said, "Ms. Frenkel, thank you for never giving up on me." Teaching them transformed me, and nearly every day I think about them. It has been two years since Bobby told me about the gang. I hope he is alive and headed in a good direction. I still want to be present in my students' lives and help them improve their writing and verbal skills. How easy it is for outsiders to make generalizations about Detroit, focusing on urban decay intertwined with a general malaise. That's not what I notice, though. I see some areas in bloom, and others budding. I know that if those budding areas are given enough light, they, too, will bloom—and they'll become as powerful as a Motown song.

In that last anthology, I also included a farewell letter:

### A Letter to Students

Chances are this will be the last time we will all be learning poetry together. I say "we" because I have learned so much from you. It has been a privilege and a joy to teach you these past three years. Please remember what remarkable talents spring forth from your writing and the safe haven writing provides. Never forget that literature is something readily available—good reading and good writing are things you can always access. And don't forget how much correct English elevates you and can improve your life!

Wherever you wind up, always kindle your curiosity and desire to read and write. Recall the magic of poetry and bring it forth. Once you enter the world of the written word in order to create it, you can create any world you choose. The miracle is that this world—which originated in your mind—then influences the material world, and who knows where your talents, desires, and dreams will take you?

With love and gratitude, I thank you. I have been blessed to call you my students and to have worked with the devoted staff and faculty at Henry Ford Academy.

CINDY FRENKEL

I wept as I wrote it.

# Where the Word Is

*Aricka Foreman*

> *We read poems because they change us, and our reasons for writing them hover*
> *around that same fact . . . Surely, as poets, most of us have discovered ways of*
> *"letting go" enough to embolden whatever it is that sends words and questions and*
> *inklings out from that space. And the best readers know that that place is where*
> *poems go when they hit us hard, teach us, reach home.*
> Tracy K. Smith, "Survival in Two Worlds at Once:
> Federico Garcia Lorca and Duende"

I return to this notion again and again, as a way of looking at process. I want to mean solely the writing process, but I think I mean the process of accepting what it means to be human. I spent a great deal of my time learning how to be an educator at InsideOut Literary Arts, and the students who have impacted me as a writer and an educator are countless. They have given me the opportunity to see the world in a different light: one full of joy and triumph, one full of real talk and hardship. But, ultimately, it's the bravery that keeps me on my path as a writer, as an advocate for creating a space in which some of us (and hopefully most) can learn that our interior is a beautiful, sacred thing.

I came to InsideOut fresh out of the corporate world where vulnerability and insight are not heralded as much as productivity and results. In the era of test scores and benchmarks, I think I needed new life breathed into me as much as my students needed to have their brilliance reflected back at them. It's the longest "job" I've kept to date, and I think that has everything to do with the work that InsideOut demands: see yourself, honestly. Write it down. Share with the world.

In 2011, I had the opportunity to work with iO's Citywide Poets Detroit Youth Slam Team, whose members consisted of Joseph Verge, Ariana Washington, Andrew Barnhill, Devin McGee, Justin Rogers, and Breana Blackmon. When I say these are some of the most beautiful poets I've had the privilege to work with, there's no limit to how understated that phrase is. I walked into one of their first practice sessions, feeling the frustration that all writers feel: that the work is not doing what we want it to. My first order of business: everyone take a break. Shake out their limbs and think of what brought them here. What made them write that poem for that person, and what was the best way we, as citizens, as writers, could honor their life with our offering? Just as importantly, how could we honor ourselves, with integrity and bravery, the gift of seeing more deeply into ourselves and our place in the world?

What transpired over the next few weeks I call magic, and those students call good *juju*, though I think there is no English translation for what developed. It was not without its long, late hours, its labor over every word, and line, and image. These students stayed hours after practice was over, careening their perspective past "confessional." Ariana was able to dig into and reconcile (on some level) the loss of her mother; Breana, the limitations of her relationship to and with her parents; Andrew and Joseph, the loss and grievance(s) of their fellow friends/brothers; Devin, who wanted to stake a claim of/for himself in every sense of the word/world. And Justin, so much hope and challenge for the city he loves, for the man he hopes to become, inspired by/in spite of it.

With my colleague and co-coach Isaac Miller, something rare took place. Isaac kept us on task, helping us to tap into a crucial performance of the text; and I just wanted us to dig, dig, dig with our pens. We each pushed one another to the edge (and beyond) of what we expected, and what others expected out of us. For the team, it was learning to let go of the confines of what the "finished" draft holds. Nothing is ever finished, but what is possible is a mirror that shows both our flaws and what we are destined to claim as our own beauty.

During the competition in the Bay area, we borrowed a Berkeley lecture hall to get ourselves ready for the first day's bout. My request was and wasn't simple: just spit the poem the way you want it to reach inside each individual audience member: to the core, the very organ of their being. Joseph got on stage to do his poem for his lost friend Jamar, a peer who was lost to complicated violence, beget by

Jamar's father's suspicion and powerlessness, beget by the way multiple communities see how justice should be carried out:

> My Dad hasn't been around in years
> But Jamar's murder makes me believe
> that God took me out my father's life to save mine
> I wonder if the day after Jamar died
> did guilt shoot through his father's mind
> like the bullet he put through his own son's head?
> His dad pulled the trigger
> in an open field surrounded by neighbors
> No one said anything
> They all stood outside of the fence
> waiting for the person next to them to call 911
> This isn't just another story I saw on TV
> This is an ode
> To a boy
> To a friend
> To a brother
> Who always wanted to get higher in life
> but was shot way further than what we all expected
> Jamar died in autumn
> The season where leaves fall and are left on the ground to die
> I never expected him to go through the same cycle
> as his body lay there, in that field
> Clenching his fist tight
> Because dignity was the only thing he had left to hold onto

There's an empathy to Joseph's poem; one that isn't precious, but curious, urgent, and challenging, in a way that reminds me of James Baldwin and his critical approach to intersections of identity and suffering from a place of hard love. This poem and its performance is necessary. Part of the way through the first third of it, his voice began to crack a bit. And though he wanted to stop; to collect himself and then go on, he did something I have rarely seen, and have few times been able to do myself: open the door to let the uncomfortable in; sit with it; receive what it wants; and release it through the work.

I've witnessed the undoing of a poem a few times, though it was here, in this mostly empty auditorium, the energy surrounding these slight seven bodies with a palpable power, that shook us all to our bones. And though I was proud of what he helped create, what he tapped into and took away, I was completely in awe. And damn, didn't I want to learn how to do THAT kind of work?

This moment was an epoch, and invited the rest of us to sacrifice something to this space. And one by one, each of the poets gave of themselves in the most bare and honest ways, each of them reached for the seed of something burrowed deep within and allowed all who witnessed to see its bloom, even if for a little while. This is what InsideOut does. Though it provides a doorway, the method of the organization and its teaching artists goes beyond that. It creates a safety net of hands for each student to reach for when they come out of the wilderness. This is not to say InsideOut saves anyone, but it provides the space for process: the chance and time to figure out each writer's power, and how to reflect it to the world.

That year we placed fourth in the festival's competition, a landmark in a couple of ways: Detroit had not placed on the final stage in some years, for the adult team or the youth team. And all of these students were either seniors in high school or first-year college students. They were a group of firsts. That summer, they fundraised harder than any one person I've ever seen. They showed up for their team and for themselves, even when they were tired, sick, or dealing with personal tragedies. They taught me what it means to be a person who, at times, has nothing left but the page, and the words, and the raw, tattered heart. When I say they WERKED, they did. The poets were overjoyed at their accomplishment, as was I because they all knew and respected the energy, focus, and deftness they crafted inside the process: that it's a malleable thing, that it demands going through the fire, and survival resides on the other side. And though it should go without saying, if they had come in last I would've been proud. It's not about slam; it's about "sending words and questions and inklings out from that space. And the best readers know that that place is where poems go when they hit us hard, teach us, reach home." Home is where the word is.

# Mess Making

*francine j. harris*

I think it's the mess of poems that allows me to work with high school students. Even though that messiness is the one thing that is most difficult to convey—how a poem can be built of anything, but how it also has to have a kind of solid structure, some sort of frame to hold it together, like any building. Teaching this is a strange process. Sure, there are ways to get to it: line, image, sound. That's what we teach. But sometimes when a poem works, you can't name what's working. It's just got that thing. Some people would call it *duende*, others call it *soul*.

But no matter what you call it, it's nothing you can put into a succinct definition on a chalkboard. Once upon a time, in the land of rhyme and scansion, I think we believed we could. But free verse has made defining wilder. There's so much ground to cover. Mood and voice and timing and off-rhyme. Defying expectations. Taking startling turns. Doing the unexpected. Doing what can't be explained. That's how you get to a good poem.

It's funny. I've had people tell me, instruct me actually, not to try to teach kids how to scan a line or to do anything with formal meter because they won't hear it. That hasn't been my experience. My experience is that if you show a young person how a poem is a big, messy pot of stuff you are just trying to get a handle on, they get that. You tell them cook in some image and some repetition and some song and some slant rhyme. If you propose that prosody and meter, like image and rhyme, is just one more ingredient—like carrots (some stews need them, some stews don't) then they'll be open to it. And I've worked with kids who actually requested we do more lessons in scansion. That threw me. I didn't tell them they'd just requested more broccoli. We just opened the pot and stirred.

That's the coolest thing about contemporary poetry to me—you can teach it a lot like you can teach someone how to cook. Sometimes you use the recipes that require all the special bakeware and brine and layering. And other times you just turn up the heat on a well-oiled pan and freestyle with whatever's in the fridge. Sometimes you get magic that way. These lines from Norman Shepherd at Mumford High remind me of that:

I put in my magic box . . .

A peanut
And out came a new way of life

The thing is, some of this mess making happens before you ever get to the page. There are poems that never see the anthologies. Snippets of lines. Freestyle moments of breakthrough. Or maybe more importantly, there are connections you make with kids who, in turn, get to work with people who take their art seriously and make a living doing so. The permission it gives them to take their own writing seriously is not lost on them. But the process of teaching writing is about as messy as the process of making poems. Every week I go in with a recipe book and every week I feel like we've come out with a dish I didn't exactly mean for us to make.

Sometimes the poem happens in a classroom without any writing happening at all. When you get to ask a kid what they think about a poem, or about themselves, or about things going on in the world. A lot of the magic is off the page. That "Magic Box" poem came from the year I worked at Mumford in 2009, the year after President Obama was elected. There was so much energy and joy in the air that year. I remember being surprised, not only that the high school kids were excited to write about the new president, but that they "got it."

Like Norman got it:

I put in hundreds of years of oppression
And out came a black president

I put in a bee
And out came a flower full of nectar
The sweetest thing on earth

Norman who seemed, in class, so cool, reserved. One of those young people I wished I could have followed. He took everything in stride. He got the mess of poems, that stuff we love, the wildness, the unanchored, the freshly excavated. There's nothing like that.

Still, there are poems that resonate the process, that somehow reflect the work we have done in class. When Jonathan Hosey at Detroit School of Arts showed me "My Last Words Before My Epitaph is Written," (see page 123 for the full poem) I felt like I saw a different side of him. Jonathan is always so sober in class and so very logical. His is a voice of reason.

He is a sweet and warm young man who always seems to have it together. He was a good writer when we started working together, which is why he made the Citywide Poets team. But I think the messy part meant a lot to Jonathan's creativity. I think it's safe to say he found a way to cut loose in his poems, to explore other possibilities. And that is, I think, the best we can do: open more doors. In this poem, Jonathan embarks upon an unwieldy adventure that begins with REM sleep. "The phase in my dreams," he says, "where they're no longer in my hands." I've often thought teaching poetry would be easier if we were all asleep. There'd be so much less resistance to the strange backdrop of poems. The poem as a phase where our imagination is no longer in our hands. Where we turn it over to the poem.

"My Last Words" is a kind of turned-over poem, a stream of consciousness that meanders along a cityscape in order to explore a simple thought: "I've come to realize that I'm succeeding in my life when I live in a society that doesn't expect me to succeed."

And that's the beautiful thing about working with young people. They so often write things to inspire themselves and others. I'm moved by how much structure young people like, by how much they want to communicate. Their poems don't alienate, or leave behind. They are not likely to write the poems that allude to old, ancient texts a lot of people don't remember. They tend to want to bring their readers along. When they play, they tend push it back toward function.

*Say I can't, I won't, I dare you. I did, I do, and I will.*

If I go in offering these young folks a way to think about getting weirder and wilder, it's the young people who remind me to bring it home. They remind me that poems can convey something, can communicate, can resolve.

That relationship—between the artist and young student—is so fantastic. I love the tension. I love that I leave every class feeling like I've suggested, encouraged, and, yes, learned.

# To Love Something

*Kristine Uyeda*

> *Teaching is just a way of modeling how to love something.*
> Patrick Rosal

I am a writer. *I am a writer.* These are words that, for many years, I was afraid or ashamed to declare. To be a writer was my most secret wish when I was twelve years old—a desire fed by my mother's collection of classic mysteries, Jane Austen novels borrowed from the Redford Branch of the Detroit Public Library, and poems like Alfred Tennyson's "The Lady of Shalott."

Now, the best of my days are spent as a writer in classrooms in Detroit teaching others to write their own poems. I listen to students read poems by well-known poets and poems that they craft themselves in class. My job is to believe. To believe absolutely that every young writer has a great poem in them—one whose joy is almost unbearable or one that drives a reader to her knees with its terrible beauty. I open small doors into vast or confining rooms, ask students to come in and dwell there for a while, bring what they wish, take what they must, and be fearless about it. Then it's my job to get out of the way and let them do their work.

When the students have their task in hand and begin writing, every sheet of paper becomes a sacred space. I move through the quiet of the room, answering questions or helping a student who feels he has nothing to say. Some students fidget while others are still and unreachably far away, listening for a poem distant but approaching more quickly with each word they write. Over their shoulders, I read what blossoms on the page: "Poetry is like knocking on my own door," "Dance with your mom, scream / until you make ends meet," "a man is planting the moon, / digging up the light."

"Ms. U., you really love it when everybody's quiet, don't you?" a student asks one day in the middle of time set aside for writing. The observation catches me off guard because I don't believe in the silent classroom. "Yes . . . and no," I reply. "This is my favorite part of class not because it's quiet but because right now, while you guys are thinking about your poems and what you have to say, everything in the world is possible." "Everything?" another student asks. "Everything," I affirm. "Time travel, new words the world hasn't even thought of yet, understanding someone you thought you didn't like very much. That's the power of writing. Everything is possible." A young man looks down at his paper and I see him cross out what he's written. When I ask him what he didn't like about it, he says enthusiastically, "It wasn't big enough!" Indeed. Poems might be small on paper but they are not small things.

After a few years of working with high school students, I am offered an assignment as a writer-in-residence to work with five sections of seventh grade students in their Social Studies classroom. We will spend our time together entering history through the lenses of art, music, and poetry. All my loves converge.

The students and I spend our first day getting to know each other and collaborating on guidelines for a safe, respectful environment. I ask them to come up with between three and five guidelines by which we will show respect and appreciation to everyone in the room. The one rule for this activity is that the guidelines should tell us how to be, as opposed to what not to do. By way of example, I offer "don't run in the hallway" versus "walk in the hallway." The first suggestion is "Don't talk!" Other students glance over disapprovingly but before someone can object, I say, "That's a great start. How can we make it sound more like it's telling us how to be?" Students offer suggestions and eventually, we get around to *listening*. I ask them for more. "What kind of listener should we each be?" The consensus in the room is that "be a good listener" should be our first guideline. From there, the list comes together quickly: sit up and give eye contact to someone who's talking, clap when someone reads his or her poem, share your supplies. The period ends. I fold up the large sheet that contains the guidelines for the class that I will print on colored paper for each student to keep in his folder. Not bad work for the first day—we've begun building our writing community, revised our work, and made the guidelines by which we'll practice being good to each other.

Two days later, I visit again and we begin making poems. I ask students what makes poems interesting. Hands pop up: "metaphors," "similes," "vivid language." We read "Dear Empire [these are your temples]" by Oliver de la Paz, and I announce that we are going to write a poem like it. The levels of excitement and skepticism rival each other. "But," I say, "we're each only going to contribute one line. And there will be some rules."

Students divide into small work groups, and I distribute strips of paper and markers. I ask for someone to tell me about metaphor and simile. Eyes flash, hands dart up and flicker. Several students hover over their desks, leaning forward for attention. I call on a student in the back of the room. The other students deflate and settle back into their seats. "A simile is a comparison of two things," he says. Immediately, hands go up again. Before calling on the next person, I thank the student for getting us started and ask, "What more could we say about simile?" A young woman corrects, "You have to use *like* or *as* when you compare them." I repeat, "A simile is a comparison of two things using *like* or *as*. What about metaphor?"

Once we've discussed what makes a metaphor, I ask for some examples. The energy in the room shifts. Coming up with examples takes some work. I suggest students look around the room for something to use in their metaphor or simile. Some students are sitting calmly while other are searching the room anxiously for something out of which to build a metaphor or simile. "Someone has one. I can feel it. Who's got one?" I ask, looking around. A student raises his hand tentatively, smiling mischievously. "My pencil is as gnawed up as an old dog bone." He holds up his pencil for the class to see. It is truly as gnawed up as an old bone. Everyone laughs. And suddenly, the window shade is an eyelid blinking, a teacher is a roaring lion when kids talk too much, the history book is as heavy as a cement block. This is often how poetry begins—one student peers quickly through the keyhole, another turns the doorknob, and then someone else gets brave enough to enter.

Eventually, we will turn our attention to ideas about what work is, the industrialization of Detroit, the Mexican muralist movement, the Blues and Jazz, and slavery in America, but today, they are in the midst of studying about Ancient Egypt, so that's where we begin. The initial goal is simple: to write four lines on a sheet of paper. Each line will begin with *I am* followed by: *a boat, the Pharaoh, the breadmaker,* or *the silt.* Each has to contain a metaphor or simile. When they are done, I ask students to choose their two most unusual lines and write each in marker on a strip of paper. Then the poem-building begins in earnest.

The groups choose an addressee, *Dear Pyramid* or *Dear Nile,* and work to assemble the lines into a poem that their group will share with the class. The noise level rises, students agree and disagree with the choices others make. Some advocate for their favorite line to be used, some have no idea what to make of all this fuss. When it's time to share the work, each group presents their poem. Here is one such poem:

**Dear Nile**
**A Collaborative Poem by Homeroom 201,**
**Clippert Academy, Detroit**

Dear Nile,

I am the boat, your heart
shivers me, glistening and slithering
underneath, the shimmering bright
emeralds are shining. I sparkle down
your blue, shine like a diamond.

I am the boat that carries the Pharaoh
while the sounds of your water lap
against the reeds that made the very boat.
It is the same color as the skies
of the Pharaoh's star. The waves,
like a desert sand flailing against
camels, stand no chance. I am the boat
that carries the Pharaoh, the morning
and evening star. The one lifted upon
the shoulders of Egypt. The one they once
called god.

There is snapping, clapping, high-fiving, and laughter. Just before the bell, students gather up and turn in all the strips on their tables, making sure to mark their names wherever there is an undisturbed stretch of white.

After class, I read through the strips of paper that contain responses to the prompt, half of which were not included in the group poems. It is difficult to go slowly, to not be in a hurry, to resist peeking around the corner. Even on this first day, the students startle me with language's unexpected possibility. *Your heart shivers me, glistening and slithering underneath, the shimmering bright emeralds are shining,* one student writes about a boat sailing down the Nile River. Another says, *I sparkle down your blue, shine like a diamond.* I am envious of this music, this magic.

*Teaching is just a way of modeling how to love something.* My heart shivers. They are twelve years old and unafraid to love strange language and new ideas. They—it turns out—are teaching me.

# Is a Change Gonna Come?

*Isaac Miller*

In my four years of working as a writer-in-residence with InsideOut I have read and heard more poems than many people do in a lifetime. I consider this to be a blessing, but more important than the volume of my students' poetry is its quality; and in turn my uncountable moments of shock, surprise, and awe when a student shares something utterly unexpected and undeniably brilliant. One thing that working with InsideOut has taught me is that you cannot pre-judge the intelligence or talent of a young person, as unfortunately many adults (myself included) too commonly do. There have been so many times when a student that I had discounted as checked-out, bored, or obstinately unwilling to write turned around and created a poem that was so compelling it stunned the classroom into silence.

In selecting a poem to write about for this anthology I was forced to consider the hundreds—if not thousands—of poems that my students have written, and while I think that there are certain poems that I hold a particular fondness for, I am inclined to think of them not as singular entities, but as part of a patchwork, strung together across classrooms, schools, and years, but united by their common origin in the voices of Detroit's youth. Above all, I believe it is important to view these voices as a movement, not only in Detroit, but in this case absolutely of Detroit, where young people are embracing poetry as a living tradition which they are taking part in rather than seeing poetry as a rarified object that must be viewed from a distance, behind protective glass.

I am certain that Writers in the Schools programs such as InsideOut are a crucial source of poetry's resurgence and its democratization in classrooms and communities across this country. I myself was brought to poetry through participating in precisely one of these spaces, the youth poetry slam festival Brave New Voices. Growing up in a small city in northern California I knew nothing about contemporary poetry and had never met a poet until I began participating in a youth literary arts program in my hometown (in a typical younger brother move I followed in the footsteps of my older brother, who had started writing poetry the year before me). Through this program I attended Brave New Voices as a thirteen-year-old, and I have been writing and reading poetry without cease ever since.

What was so electrifying about Brave New Voices was the way it offered living proof that poetry, a thousands-year-old tradition, was something that I could take part in as a young person alive today in this very moment. Because of Brave New Voices my friends were poets, my heroines and heroes were poets, my teachers and mentors were poets. This is an entirely different relationship to poetry than the way that (for the most part) our schools have approached the teaching and learning of the poetic tradition. This is not the fault of teachers, many of whom have themselves been trained to handle poetry with surgical gloves, but it reinforces a relationship of distance (if even that) to an art form that is as intimate and vital as a heartbeat.

One thing I love about InsideOut is that it brings the kind of experiences that I had at Brave New Voices (a once-a-year festival) into classrooms throughout Detroit on a weekly basis. Poetry is woven into the curriculum in a way that I never experienced growing up. As a result I believe this work is shifting the way an entire generation will view poetry as something to be celebrated rather than something to be feared. I don't think we will see the full effects of the work of InsideOut and its sister organizations for some time (it is not easily quantified on a standardized test), but I know what a difference it has made in my life and in the lives of so many young people.

All of that being said, as much as I deeply love working in classrooms as a writer-in-residence, I have to say that the high point of my time with InsideOut was the summer that I had the honor of co-coaching InsideOut's Citywide Poets Youth Poetry Slam Team. Along with my colleague Aricka Foreman I was one of two coaches that worked with the team's six youth poets in preparation for the Brave New Voices International Youth Poetry Slam Festival, held that year in San Francisco. That summer was one of the most demanding moments of my career as a teaching artist, with the team practicing and writing together several times a week, performing throughout Detroit, emailing drafts of their poems out on Google Docs, and revising, revising, revising.

The result of the team's hard work was a portfolio of extraordinarily vivid poems, all of which will live in my head for years to come. However, though Aricka and I believed in the team with our utmost, I would be lying if I said it didn't take my breath away when they made the finals of Brave New Voices. Out of fifty teams from all over the United States and around the world, only four teams made the finals stage that year at the San Francisco Opera House. One of those teams was Detroit and their performance that night moved me (and many others) to tears.

While I would be hard-pressed to pick a favorite poem from that year's team, because they were all of such intelligence, maturity, creativity, and heart, there is one poem in particular that I have reflected on quite a bit since that festival in the summer in 2011. That poem is called "Change," and it was written by Breeana Blackmon, then a high school senior. The poem is a response to the unmet expectations of Obama's presidency and the change for which so many of us hoped.

The poem begins,

Yes We Can
The crowd goes wild
I hear screams from here to there
Smiles similar to those of small children
plastered onto adult faces
And the whole time
I'm wishing I had a megaphone so loud
people in the far corners of every country
can hear me say
No We Can't.

Breeana reminds us of the moment in November 2008 when it seemed as if an impossible hurdle had been overcome, the first African American president of a country whose original constitution would not have recognized him as a full human being. And yet, despite this momentous event, what really had changed?

She writes:

> On Election Day people stood in line for hours
> with their children and great-grandmothers
> to put their name in the box marked hope.
> So they could say they were a part of history,
> together.
>
> They woke up the next morning
> to the same prostitutes, hungry children, and dope men
> that were there the day before,
> went on about their day without guilt
> because they knew it'd get better.
> After all, they voted.
> The new president will save them.
>
> Insanity is doing the same thing repeatedly
> and expecting a different outcome.
> Things don't sporadically change
> because a man with brown skin
> made it into a white palace
> off a catchy campaign.
> It's gonna take more than one man
> to bring justice to a country that wasn't even built on it.

Breeana's poem brings to mind the words of the 98-year-old Detroit philosopher-activist Grace Lee Boggs, who wrote, "Our challenge now is to recognize that the future of our country and our planet is as much about us as about Obama, that in our communities and our cities we have become responsible for grappling with the issues he is wrestling with."[1]

In Breeana's poem she struggles with the question of what it will actually take to achieve the change we believed in, which she makes clear has always required far more challenging and courageous work than any campaign slogan can convey:

> We've come this far because poets used to scream on street
>     corners,
> movements used to be about a million men
> marching to the rhythm of their heartbeats.
> Their footsteps sent out vibrations
> that made people's minds shift to a different position.
> People used to die for what they believed in.

Ultimately, Breeana's poem is about a radical sense of self-reliance. This is not self-reliance in the conservative sense of the term, which in fact depends on the government to provide subsidies and tax breaks that privilege the most wealthy and powerful in our society at the expense of the most vulnerable. The sense of self-reliance that I hear in Breeana's poem is one that believes that the people of Detroit have the power to solve the problems that face them. These are solutions that no politician or corporation can provide, but must come from the people themselves:

> This is about more than scraping up pennies and nickels
> to pay city officials
> to do what we can already do
> just by individually deciding
> that we are gonna make it our business to save ourselves.
> We have to drop dimes and quarters worth of time and
>     compassion
> into our community piggy banks.
> Maybe then we might mess around
> and get ourselves a dollar.

Though Breeana utilizes money as a metaphor in the ending of her poem, I read this as expressing an idea much deeper than simply achieving monetary wealth. Once again, I hear an echo of Grace Lee Boggs, who writes that, in the context of climate change and widening economic disparity, the "next American Revolution" is about "living the kind of lives that will not only slow down global warming but also end the galloping inequality both inside this country and between the Global North and the Global South. . . . It is about practicing a new, more active, global, and participatory concept of citizenship. It is about becoming the change we wish to see in the world."[2] This is precisely the kind of change that Breeana's poem speaks to, and that undeniably needs to be heard.

## Notes

1. Grace Lee Boggs and Scott Kurashige, *The Next American Revolution* (Berkeley: University of California Press, 2011), 165.

2. Boggs and Kurashige, 72.

# However You May Say It

*Kristin Palm*

> Detroit just sits there
> like the head of a large dog on a serving platter. . . .
> Air the color of brown Necco wafers,
> a taste like the floor of an adult movie theater,
> the movement through the streets
> that of a legless, wingless pigeon. . . .

The poem, read out loud, draws laughter, like many poems that have come before. For the past six months, I have spent one day a week teaching students at Detroit's Southeastern High School to write poetry. Today, the assignment is to discuss Jim Gustafson's poem "The Idea of Detroit," then use metaphor to write two original pieces: "The Idea of Detroit" (the city as seen by others) and "My Idea of Detroit."

I begin by simply writing the word "Detroit" on the board and asking the students to shout out images that come to mind: crackheads, booty, Belle Isle, fried chicken, hot boys, Motown, Macktown, Tigers . . . the list goes on. Next, we read Gustafson's poem, concluding with the lines: "Detroit just sits there / drinking can after can of Dupe beer, / checking the locks on the windows, / sighing deeply, knowing that nothing / can save it now." I ask the students who they think wrote this poem. "Someone from the suburbs," they say. Actually, I tell them, Gustafson was a well-known poet and journalist who lived in the Cass Corridor. The students are puzzled. "Remember, the title is 'The Idea of Detroit,'" I tell them. The students nod their heads. Aha.

After some brainstorming, I ask the kids to write their own "Idea" poems. The following week, we compile the strongest lines into one group piece.

*Kristin Palm*

## Up and Down in D-Town

*(after Jim Gustafson's "The Idea of Detroit")*

Detroit/D-Town/The Motor City
However you may say it

Detroit sits
like field rats on top of garbage cans,
a baby's mama at the end of her rope,
the lumpiness of Woodward,
the Renaissance
and whatever else is left

Detroit/D-Town/The Motor City
However you may say it

Detroit is Rolex spelled with an "N"
It's lost under wallpaper,
stands alone like a bag of ice
at the grocery store in winter

Detroit/D-Town/The Motor City
However you may say it

Detroit is the junk on the bottom of your shoe.
It smells like a thousand McDonald's bathrooms,
like boys after a basketball game,
like clothes you haven't washed for weeks.

Detroit/D-Town/The Motor City
However you may say it

Detroit is the Godfather
Bustin' for real, playin' for keeps
Detroit rocks after hours

Detroit/D-Town/The Motor City

However you may say it

Detroit is a game of dressup,
a night of cards,
jump rope in the afternoon,
a million-dollar mansion

Detroit/D-Town/The Motor City
However you may say it

Detroit is a rocky roller coaster ride,
a cruise on a jet-propelled speed boat,
jumping out of a plane at two hundred thousand feet,
a yo-yo yanking up
        and down
           and up
             and down
               and . . .

Detroit/D-Town/The Motor City
However you may say it

Detroit is still standing

Detroit is still standing

Detroit is still standing

I am impressed, though not surprised, that the students have so ably grasped the contradictions of the city. I witnessed this same keen perception when they wrote about their neighborhoods and about art. What amazes me, however, is that when they read their poem out loud, they all sense that something is not quite right. They're uncomfortable with the ending, it turns out. This is your piece, I tell them. What do you want to do? First, they suggest cutting "Detroit is still standing." But it still doesn't feel quite right. Then Iris comes up with the clincher:

Detroit/D-Town/The Motor City
However you may say it

Detroit is a rocky roller coaster ride,
a cruise on a jet-propelled speed boat,
jumping out of a plane at two hundred thousand feet,
a yo-yo yanking up
         and down
             and up
                   and down
                      and . . .

Detroit/D-Town/The Motor City
However YOU may say it

Same refrain, different emphasis. To some, such a small shift may seem insignificant. But, as poets know, one subtle twist can make all the difference. This is a performance piece, and I'm pleased that the students understand that it's not just what you say, but how you say it. And to whom. In the end, they turn their refrain into a challenge, a bold, East Side, "Come and say that to my face!" And their poem is no longer just about how they, or others, see Detroit. It's a poem about how they see the outsiders who see the city. These kids know that history has been unkind not only to Detroit, but to them because they live here. With this poem, they have created a way of seeing the city—and themselves in the city—that gives them power and agency. And that is what this exercise, that is what writing poetry, is all about.

# Notes for that Screenplay One of Us Needs to Write

*Stacy Parker Le Melle*

**1.**

This kind of silence is not stillness. This kind of silence is charged and dense and if you work hard it fills you as a teaching artist, it floats you as you walk down each aisle, or behind the backest back row, once you've reached the point in your lesson when it's time for your students to write.

For you did more than ask your students to write. You asked them to braid together ideas, to take the brainstorming, the model poem, the CD recording of a Citywide Poets performance—the whatever it is you shared with them that day to stir up their memories and observations and offer them up as reflections, maybe even art. You asked them to bring poetic order to the inner storm. You created a classroom space where, if they're brave, they can sit with themselves and visit and listen to those feelings and words that would remain otherwise suppressed.

And they do! This kind of silence is the sound of every student thinking and moving a pencil across the paper. And not just your usual participants. All of the kids. The quiet ones. The loud ones. The sleepers. The "I don't understands." For, at this blessed moment in time, everyone understands. Down Jefferson Avenue, the assembly liners build cars one part at a time, and across the neighborhood grid, the postmen and women deliver mail house by house. But on this morning, at Southeastern High School, the students tell their truths in graphite strokes and the silence is beautiful and alive. You take an empty seat. You soak it in. This is success.

**2.**

Years later, in my Harlem apartment, I will watch my three-year-old son stack alphabet blocks. One on top of another. My son is a tall little kid, and his stack reaches up to his shoulders. He carefully

places the last block atop the just-shuddering column and boom—
the whole thing crashes to bits. He laughs. Time to do it again.

It wasn't always like this. I bought those blocks when he was
a one-year-old. Back then, all he wanted to do was gnaw on their
wooden edges. When he could finally put one block atop another, he
cried when pieces fell down. Sometimes he wanted to throw them.
Sometimes he did throw them. He needed to build, and fail, before
he could build and succeed. This took several months. He didn't
build tall stacks with ease until he was three.

Yet I often buy toys and think, yes, we will hand them to our son,
and *voila*, he will know exactly what to do. This, despite being an educator. This, despite knowing, intellectually, that one has to learn how
to do something, that it's silly to secretly desire that our children will
be able to do anything correctly on a first try. To be good at something, anything, we have to practice. Again. And again. My son had to
learn that if the blocks fall, he can pick them up and start over. That
there is no crisis. That he can build again. That he can build higher.

**3.**

When I remember teaching in that Detroit classroom, I know I was
proud. But only now do I realize that I was too proud. I misunder-
stood something crucial about that silence: that whatever we reaped
in that class hour was first sown by years of assigned and completed
writing assignments, of readings in class and outside of class, by all
that the students observed and were asked to comprehend and engage, by the cultivation of curiosity itself—in short: by all of the work
done before we, the teaching artist, ever stepped into their worlds.

How could I have been so blind? I never fully saw the importance
of the daily work. For if I had understood this fact in a felt way, I
would have known then to credit my students' teachers and parents
even more than I did.

No previous hard work = no teaching artist success.

**4.**

There's a silence that is also erasure. There is nothing sweet or electric about it, and the erasure blinds even those convinced of their
strong vision.

Consider the Hollywood "inner-city teacher done good" films. Who plays the star teachers? Sidney Poitier. Michelle Pfeiffer. Edward James Olmos. Perfectly fine actors: all of them earning their places in the pantheon of Hollywood greats. But here is my trouble: none of those men or women mirror the teaching protagonists of my own life experiences. The star public school teachers I worked with were not supermodel blondes or patriarchs taking charge—they were mostly middle-aged and older women, a mix of black and white, who had devoted their lives to the education of children. This was and remains my norm, my lived experience. And I've yet to see a Hollywood movie that tries to portray a successful inner-city classroom reflect this norm.

The teachers and administrators I worked with in inner-city schools, through their actions, seemed to interlock fingers and form the chain that created continuity, stability, and order for the children in their charge. They built the house that allowed for play. They did so in neighborhoods ravished by poverty, they did so for many children who could not count on stability at home. And when a hole was blown through a wall, they worked to repair. And repair. Sometimes, I imagine these schoolhouses as hit by societal and political hurricanes, or at least strong winds, and the walls could shudder, sometimes topple, from those outside forces. But every day, I saw teachers work to maintain order and offer the love necessary for a child to feel safe enough to unclench, relax, and learn.

I think of the efforts of so many teachers: Geretha Mosby, Minnie Muhammad, Bonnie O'Brien, Elizabeth Kurtz—too many teachers to count. But I think often of Donna James at Southeastern High School in Detroit. She oversaw the English department. I have never seen her mirrored in a Hollywood movie. And because of this, the world is missing the image of the hardworking, devoted, spirit-filled Black woman who walked the walk for her inner-city students, who was excited about the work InsideOut did in the classroom, and was as supportive of my residencies as any writer could ask for. No one needed to helicopter her in to save the day. She was doing that already.

I must also speak of Cathy Williams. I worked with Cathy Williams at the now-closed Douglass Elementary School in Houston, Texas. Ms. Williams taught the fourth grade "G&T" class in a predominantly Black school in the city's Third Ward. That blessed silence? I felt it all of the time in that classroom full of attentive, eager, well-behaved students. Because of the house that Cathy Williams built, I could experiment with any lesson plan I wanted and not have to be concerned with also holding up the roof and the walls. She was my hero. Did Cathy Williams look like Michelle Pfeiffer, or for that matter, Geoffrey Canada? No. She was a big-boned white woman from Louisiana, near retirement-age. Yes, I mention her frame, for she didn't look like the Hollywood version of her vocation. Yet she was a strong, inspired presence. She had devoted her life's work to nurturing and teaching those children. I cherish my days in her classroom, when we basked in the charged silence when all of her children were writing, creating new worlds on their own.

The teachers of my own childhood, the teachers I worked with as a teaching artist, they were the blessings I never fully saw. Here's to us all opening our eyes a bit wider, especially those of us proud of our vision. That way, we can see better all of the shoulders upon shoulders that hold us up, let us do our work in the world.

**5.**

One last note: When you cast actors for this film, remember that the teaching artists came from all kinds of backgrounds. Some were born in the inner city and some were born in the outer neighborhoods, and none of these poets needed to be taught what was vibrant in Detroit City. Some grew up downriver, brought the stars and moon and mud to the classroom every day. Some grew up in the suburbs, took a look around at the newness, at the inequalities, and wanted to make things right. So keep that in mind, please. When flipping through headshots, you must look for beautiful people. But not the sameness of cutout dolls, please. The beauty of the teaching artists, the students, the school principals—this beauty radiates first from the heart, then from the eyes and from the sounds of their voices, from their stories and poems. Remember how diverse they are: Black, White, Asian, Hispanic, and Mixed in a hundred gorgeous ways. The ages will range from elementary to elderly, and there will be beauty in all of their faces. If you cast this film like InsideOut Literary Arts Project's Terry Blackhawk has staffed her teams, your motion picture will be luminous. And if you take notes from what my former colleagues said in class, or in conversation? Your script will be golden. Just remember: practice. Montages of practice and of all that came before our teaching assignments. And then montages of all of the writing we did in a single year. If you include those, your script will be full of quiet triumph. The kind that makes you sit back in awe, the kind that makes you know what success really feels like.

**Impossible Is Nothing**
**Richard Littleton**
**Southeastern High School**
**2007**
This blessing poem is for those
who don't think impossible is nothing.
Well impossible is nothing we all
can achieve something.

The problems that you have are
denial and low self-esteem.
Don't mind the backstabbing, just
look and bounce like a trampoline.
Show the world what you got
don't put it in storage,
show some pride, don't have lack of
courage.

The dreams you have are being the
greatest and not failing,
so pass your own test
just get up and take a chance, show
people you're the best.

But I do admire your dignity and
your heart,
don't hold your head down, you were
great from the start.

Watch me, I could show you something.
To be a believer and that
impossible is nothing.

I'll show you how to do the impossible
and how to be stunning.
I want to show you that impossible is
nothing.

# I Named You the Honeycomb

*Alise Alousi*

A boy by the name of Dominique was my favorite student the year I was pregnant. He tried to make my life miserable for the first few weeks, proclaiming every model poem boring and my writing prompts laugh-out-loud funny. I learned a lot that year about how being consistently open to change can disrupt a pattern. That was an idea that would come in handy with a baby that cried for six months straight. Dominique didn't write much that year, which isn't to say he didn't work hard for every word he did write. He called me over to his desk at least once each lesson, *Miss Alise, Miss Alise, How does this sound?* Reading me a line or two at a time.

One day he labored over several lines that became the epigraph to the Cody literary journal that year. They were so much of what Dominique was all about—carefully placed words that were vulnerable yet shaded with bravado. Not unlike what it feels like to be pregnant for all the world (or a room full of eleventh graders) to see.

**Black**
is
the
shadow
looking
at
you
making sure
you
are
straight.

DOMINIQUE DARNELL

At the end of my time with them, my students threw me a baby shower. They brought in gifts and snacks and made a huge card that I have to this day. They wanted to know whether it would be a boy or a girl, my plans for a name. They had seen me through an important year in my life, and working with them shored me up for being a first-time parent.

Sometimes, if you are lucky, a job can align with the trajectory of your life in a way that feels profoundly right. When I landed at iO the second time around, after taking a six-year break, I was asked to lead a series of parent workshops at Gardner Elementary, a diverse school on the west side of Detroit. As the parent of an elementary school child, I'd become aware of the mostly unnatural ways parents get thrown together in a school setting. There are parents who enter and exit their child's school with ease and confidence but the vast majority don't, and this barrier can affect whether they feel empowered to advocate for and support their child educationally.

Something that had stayed with me from my work in other nonprofits is the idea that parents often want the same opportunities their children have; with iO this meant a shared community around writing and creative self-expression. Parents in the sessions at Gardner, all mothers, came from a variety of backgrounds religiously and ethnically—including recent refugees from Iraq, Yemen, and Africa. For the first session we read *The United Nations Rights of the Child* and the Khalil Gibran poem, "On Children."

Your children are not your children
They are the sons and daughters of Life's longing for itself
They come through you but not from you,
And though they are with you yet they belong not to you.

Parents wrote poems of address to their children modeled on the ideas in these texts. What are the rights we want our children to own? What does the world we want them to inhabit look like? What are our dreams for their futures?

For the next few workshops, I went back to some tried and true creative writing lessons. We wrote advice poems and *I remember* poems, and I realized why these lessons we fall back on work so well.

During one of the last sessions we wrote name poems. Many writers launch their residencies with this lesson based on a short piece by Sandra Cisneros in *The House on Mango Street*, and it always produces strong work. We talked about the stories behind our own names and the names we chose for our children. I shared the story of my daughter Esme's name from my lifelong love of the J. D. Salinger story "For Esme with Love and Squalor." Her name, pronounced slightly differently, also exists in Arabic and several of the mothers were familiar with this name, Asma, which means the ninety-nine names of God.

The school provided an Arabic-speaking translator for the workshops. One mother, Ashawk, from Iraq was an eager participant—always asking when I'd return for the next meeting. She shared her feelings about her own name, which she never really liked as a child, and then wrote a piece for her daughter who was born with special needs. During the previous sessions she'd written in Arabic and read her work out loud with the help of the translator. For this lesson she told me she wanted to write the poem for her daughter on her own and in English.

I named you Shahed. I named you the honeycomb.
My name has a lot of meanings. I've lived most of my life
away from my mom and brothers, my family, my friends and my
    universe.
I wanted to give you a name that would give you hope for meeting
good results in the end of every part of this life.
And for you to be a full person and patient because the way is
    long.
To taste the honeycomb after all that active work from the bee.
My sweetheart, be like the bee, get the good results the bee gets.

Here's my daughter, Esme, explaining to a younger friend what I do:

She writes poems.
*What are poems?*
Poems are like small stories.

*So she writes small stories?*
Yes, she writes small stories and she teaches kids how to write
small stories.
*Oh. My mom is a nurse. She delivers babies. Sometimes she tells me
what they got named. I think you might like a mom like mine.*

I could not help but think of Ashawk and the other mothers when I
overheard this conversation. During the series of workshops a sense
of camaraderie developed as we shared our hopes, fears, dreams and
advice with each other, free of labels and inhibition, we were simply a room full of mothers who all want the best, sweetest, lives for
their children. What a lucky place to be.

# Langston's Hues

*Chace Morris*

It's my first year at InsideOut when Alise Alousi approaches me about an opportunity to teach solo for the first time. It's an abbreviated assignment at Langston Hughes Middle School, helping a handful of sixth graders craft poems and performances for the "Get Versed" gala at the end of the year. For the greater part of the year, I had been serving as co-writer to the venerable Marcus Wicker at Cody High School where he showed me the ropes. And though working with Marcus gave me a lot of confidence, the idea of being solely responsible for a classroom of all-new students in the middle of the year within a grade level I was not accustomed to definitely increased the ol' heart rate a few considerable ticks.

That first day with the students and Ms. Rushing (their teacher) was the perfect antidote to my anxiety. I'll never forget how I came in with my clipboard covered in bullet points for all the lessons I was going to hit them with so we could generate good poems for the gala performance, only to get there and find that they each already had first drafts of killer concepts ready to go. It blew my mind! I'm talking ideas with legit emotional depth and excitement in the freedom to take risks and break rhyme schemes. It completely knocked me off my pivot and forced me to retool my approach in the best kind of way. Over the next couple weeks, my class of eight students was cut in half to a modest four (due to a myriad of reasons). But those four remaining students—Maurice, Daymond, Kristian, and Tre'zhane—were some of the most lively, most creative students I've encountered in my short time here at InsideOut.

Maurice wanted to write a tribute poem to his mother but was insistent that it had to be funny to meet his personality instead of being super-serious and dramatic. So I had him choose three very specific things that she did for (or with) him that inspired such poetic worthiness. The poem ended up centering around things like saving his life right in the nick of time in Call of Duty: Black Ops, and we focused on shaping the performance around his natural talking speed and mannerisms so that he felt more comfortable on stage with the poem and he could deliver the humor of it in a way that the crowd would respond to.

Daymond also wanted to write a poem about his mother, but his took a different turn. He used the concepts of light and darkness to tackle the deep loneliness he felt when he was without his mother, and how her presence brought that warmth back into his world. Imagery and specificity would be key here, so I had him think of a place where both light and shadow are both extremely prevalent and work the piece from there. He chose an alley at night and used that extended metaphor to flesh out the heart of the poem.

Kristian had an almost three-page poem ready to go when I first stepped foot into class. It was a very aggressive piece itemizing all of these terrible things that he'd seen in the world at such a young age, but how it's even worse not trying to fix these things and that if we don't act soon, then it may become too late. To get that type of focused, impassioned work from a sixth grader was a bit face-melting, and so we wanted to keep that tone but edit it into something shorter for the sake of making the poem a more tightly packed precision punch as opposed to swinging an axe at every generality in his experience. So I gave him one page to fit all of the most pressing issues he listed, and we ordered the piece from there so it flowed and still had the impact.

Though each of these poems hit me in different ways and really made me proud to be working with such wildly talented students, it was Tre'zhane and her poem dedicated to her grandmother that hit me the deepest. At the time, she was dealing with her grandmother's recent passing and wanted to work through it by writing a poem about what an amazing woman she was. What really got me was her willingness to break convention and describe certain things in inventive ways before we even made edits. She had all these beautiful memories she wanted to share, and when we started talking about imagery I remembered she got really excited about including some of those specifics in the poem. And in the finished piece you can see everything she wrote. You get this attachment to her grandmother in such a short amount of time, and instantly you think of that person you may have lost that meant so much to you and consequently build that connection to Tre'zhane. All that from a sixth grader!

It was my first real lesson in never underestimating the students when entering a classroom. It was an experience in learning and being moved by the student as much as going into the class trying to accomplish that yourself. That lesson, that student, and that poem have stuck with me as what can be accomplished when you join your ideas as teacher to the motives and emotions of the student as opposed to always trying to show them better.

# A Nebulous Space

*Anita Schmaltz*

Just about a year ago, back in January 2013, I received an email out of the ether from Alise Alousi, a former coworker of mine and now Associate Director of InsideOut—*former* because I had stopped teaching three years prior.

I had stopped for a junction of reasons: the challenges of teaching at three schools that year (I'd only ever done two at most before) combined with a tense relationship with a newly appointed administrator, and, most importantly, my energies were more than ever required to help care for my mother who had been struggling with Parkinson's disease for over two decades. Regardless of almost a decade of experience as a writer-in-residence, all these together led to one of those sad moments when faith is overwhelmed by doubt. I let go of teaching, and for the next few years, we—all the eyes of my family—watched my mother's deterioration until she withered away into her final peace. After the funeral, once the house I grew up in was cleared and cleaned for a new family, I found myself in need of work again.

Then I received Alise's unexpected email:

> Four of our students performed an original group piece today for an MLK event at Orchestra Place. They did an amazing job—they were poised and brilliant before an audience of close to a thousand.
>
> Afterwards one of the students, a young man named Jonathan Hosey, asked me to reach out to you. You were his writer-in-residence at Marion Law Academy. He told me, "I wouldn't be here today, I wouldn't be doing what I am doing if it were not for her."
>
> He was so earnest and sincere. I was really moved . . .

Right away, Jonathan's face flashed into my mind, and also the memory of sitting in a large room, proofreading manuscripts for publication with other writers-in-residence, and one of the writers spontaneously shouting out when reading Jonathan's poem in Marion Law Academy's second volume of *Law-e-try Po-e-try*.

**Route 95**
Fills up in the
ocean, turns to
a cloud, gets too
heavy, turns
to fog, here
comes the apple . . .

Route 95 is a magic apple
bent on world domination.
As it passes the world, it
turns citizens into slaves of
witches. The apple goes through
Barcelona, Spain's great balcony,
storms through the great tower
of Italy, destroys downtown
Hong Kong, China, causes a
drought at Niagara Falls, Canada,
follows the route of the three
magic cities after his revenge is
complete. Halloween town, Noki village
and Shell city, Pianta village
plus Bikini Bottom, the apple
goes along the Rio Grande.

JONATHAN HOSEY—2007

"Route 95" was written in response to my lesson I called *Following a Path*, a lesson I'd presented during my two-year residency at Law Academy seven years earlier, when Jonathan was in third and fourth grade. I responded to Alise's email with, "If I remember correctly, he was a better writer than me in the fourth grade," because even at that young age, it was already quite clear to me that Jonathan's abilities were far beyond his years.

Back in 2007, this fourth grader had struck me as *so* advanced and out of place, I had called a local progressive school for gifted students—Roeper Academy—on his behalf. I found out that they offered scholarships for low-income students and put together a package for Jonathan's teacher to give to his parents, including a letter of recommendation from me. I couldn't submit an application *for* him, his parents had to do that, so I did what I could. I remember a phone call from his mother, nervous about the idea and asking my advice. After that phone call, I never heard anything more about the application or Jonathan until this January.

Because of Alise's email, I began interacting with InsideOut writers again, and, soon afterwards, was asked if I'd be interested in picking up some schools, which I did last spring—three concentrated residencies before the end of the school year. I surprised myself at how quickly I picked up steam and charged through the lessons. But I could never seem to make it to one of Jonathan's performances. There always seemed to be a conflict with the date and time. This went on for months.

Last week, we met for the first time in many years at a coffee house in Detroit. The weather had just taken a dive in temperature and the whole city was shivering. I walked into the warmth and saw Jonathan, now a young man, a junior in high school, huddled over his drink in a dark, knit grey beanie. For the next two and a half hours, we went over our recent lives. When I brought up the Roeper package, he knew nothing about it. I had assumed that extra thing I did for him was behind what he'd told Alise. It turns out what I'd thought wasn't true at all.

Jonathan told me that ever since he was little, he knew he wanted to do something important. He reminded me he'd done the cover art for the first Marion Law literary magazine I'd put together. I remembered it, a black and white pencil depiction of a city: a complex overview of roads, bridges and buildings, a city hall, hospital, bank, fire department, clinic, library, pizza restaurant, and more. He'd drawn that picture because at the time I met him in third grade, Jonathan had decided he wanted to be an architect, but not anymore. He told me, "You changed the trajectory of my life." When I asked him *how?* it turned out to be because of something I do all the time: I made Jonathan share his work. He described himself as being a shy boy and was afraid to read in front of class, but because I pushed him to do it, he changed.

This shy boy now wants to be a television reporter and broadcast journalist. He auditioned and was accepted into Detroit School of the Arts and is already in his third year writing as well as assisting in the production of the teen talk show "Can You Relate" on Detroit Public Schools' Radio aired on WRCJ (90.9 FM), the first/youngest freshman to do so at DSA. Jonathan continually involves himself in community-minded groups (his participation in the Detroit Youth Green Economy Summit as an MC/facilitator in 2011 earned him the Spirit of Detroit award). He performs with DSA's choral ensemble Voices of Jubilation and InsideOut's Citywide Poets. He looks to the future, not only wanting to focus on presenting the things that affect real people, especially those unheard stories in the neighborhoods, the "whys" behind the crimes, he also wants to start a school that resolves his disappointments with Detroit Public Schools, a place of international study focusing on the arts, athletics, science and foreign language, a school to create international leaders through a well-rounded education with an emphasis on demonstration and *presentation*.

He said it again, "You changed the trajectory of my life." He said it many times.

I think he sensed I was having trouble believing him.

I told him, "Because of you, I'm teaching again."

Before we left each other, I asked Jonathan to be sure to email me some of his current writing.

**My Last Words Before My Epitaph is Written**
REM sleep
The phase in my dreams when they are no longer in my hands

It is there that I see orange skies
And everything almost sepia tone
Empty fields besides tall abandoned buildings

And my fresh-skinned young mother carrying me, a baby in her
   arms

Alone down a street not a stranger to killings
2Pac plays in our background
But when I sit in isolation creating
Listening for better words to express what my young voice has
   to say
And belting Anita Baker in the shower
It doesn't occur to me that I may be doing
Something slightly different
From what you imagine a little black boy doing
Things different from what is expected of me
A little black boy from Detroit

No, it doesn't quite occur to me
Until I sit across from a young musical prodigy
Interviewing her on her experience being date raped
Thinking how her story can be told to help other teen girls
As I strive to be taken seriously in what *I* do
I realize that I am becoming what I dream to become

It is late afternoon
I take my seat under the lighting synonymous with the hard
Evening news programs
Having put on my old pro, hard news suit
I tell the producers to prepare some tissues
I am Barbara Walters
And for the first time I will not have to wait
To come in after the man on question four
This one is all mine
I sit across from a girl a few years my senior
Leaning in with head rested on my hand, probing
Like this is 1988 and I'm getting a heart poured out to me by
   Oprah
Yes, I hope for Barbara results

I grew up being humbled by warm compliments
Knowing in truth I was born a statistic
And that society is well prepared to write my epitaph
But from the arms that carried me for dear life
I stand now
Pants at my waist
Shirt buttoned
To be the man I found in myself
The one an absent father hadn't taught me to be
But the one that I had to be

From the soul-shaking tears of ghettos
From broken glass on cracked sidewalks
From smashed liquor bottles
And a white eastside bungalow
And the first sit in that chair
Under those lights synonymous with hard news
That this black boy dares take a seat
I'll never forget my talk with you
Girl whose name we had to change to tell your story
I'll never forget the feel of that chair

JONATHAN HOSEY—2013

Last night I picked up my friend Mirinda, a lovely mystic poet *and*—I am convinced—part of the fairy kingdom. We went to the Cranbrook planetarium to see the film presentation, "The Secret Life of Stars." As we were the only ones in the domed theater for this last showing of the day, after the film the man on the microphone showered us two poets with special, *celestial* treatment. He named a blue giant in the boot of the constellation of Orion after my friend—*The Mirinda Star.* In the hunter's sword, there was now *The Anita Nebula.*

Nebulas look like solid entities but they're not, they're ghostly clusters of dust and interstellar gases. They only look solid because of all of the colored light they're bathed in, the prismatic internal changes of the stars inside them. Nebulas are nurseries for birthing new stars. And I thought, how harmonious this idea happens to be with the art of teaching—it's a sort of kaleidoscopic faith, holding within its gaseous, indefinite fingers the possibility of so many stars, so many new stars. And it's those brilliant sparks of radiant energy that color the trust that what is being taught will take shape and substance, if not today, then someday, somehow.

Toward the end of our meeting, Jonathan had asked me how the teaching was going. I told him I was having a rough start at my school and heard myself sounding doubtful as to the effectiveness of my efforts. I was complaining as if I were a voice in the dark. He let me have it.

"You're one of the best teachers I've ever had. You have an impact, even if they don't know it . . ." and he kept going, reason after reason, how I introduced him to different kinds of writing, how I brought things into the room he didn't know existed, why what I do is so important and how I should never underestimate my ability to change lives—*my* student's energy shining back on me, in a glow of multicolored mists over my doubts and shadowings.

# Split and Sprout from InsideOut

*Thomas Park*

When Terry Blackhawk interviewed me for a position as writer-in-residence at InsideOut back in 2007, I had no idea of the magnitude it would change life. It was the best contract I ever signed. I was assigned to be the writer at Southeastern and Northwestern High Schools. Man, I was scared to go to Southeastern. I was a student there in the seventh grade thirty-six years earlier and was mugged and robbed of my milk money weekly. Once, during my residency there, a kid asked me to let him "hold my phone." I told him no and was hit in the head with a snowball thrown by one of his associates. But it was all good.

Today, when I flip through the iO student publications, I am amazed with each turn of the page that I remember almost every student. Like 6'7" all-city football-star William Gholson who reluctantly wrote very beautiful poems before going on to MSU fame. Or the sophisticated lady "Sam" who skipped school once a week and wrote of high school friends who stayed well dressed by performing in neighborhood "Boom-Boom" rooms. There was Brittany C. who always wrote letters. She wanted to be able to write to her dad who, she told me, was in prison "for a long-long time." Two of the many highlights while working for iO occurred when her grandmother wrote me a stirring letter thanking me for helping her. Her father also wrote me a moving letter thanking me and InsideOut. He said that ever since his daughter had been in the writing class they had been corresponding frequently and had become very close. One could see the rapid healing of her spirit. Another big guy, D. W., used to sit and doodle; he reluctantly began to write and composed a poem that he let me read. It was to his brother who was "locked up." When I told him the poem was good writing he broke down in tears; D. W. participated every day after that.

My first nominee for one InsideOut poetry gala-banquet was a cutter, a gender-challenged, beautiful, acne-pimpled lady from a very tough environment with few resources. Students both North and South strongly identified with this young writer's poetry and were concerned for her well-being. She was unfortunately shipped off to the Job Corp. I nominated Sam to represent Southeastern; it was then I found out she only came to class on iO poetry days.

One of the most rueful days of my life was in 2009 when I decided to go back home to teach in rural North Carolina. I could not wait to start a poetry club in our high school; *County Wide* compared to *City Wide*. My star student Dameon Williams was a very reserved honor student. His big brother was also serving a long prison sentence. He had gang affiliations that he ended while in the poetry group. Dameon graduated and enrolled at Winston Salem State University. He is the first in his family to attend college. There were also standout poets Jane Groom, Gabrielle Kearney, Kaylee Roach, Alan Henderson, and José Sanchez. I mention them because I always told them they were extensions of a larger family of writers, first cousins of InsideOut Detroit.

Sometimes I would rib my North Carolina kids. I'd tell them that people always wanted to talk about how problematic and ill-mannered "inner-city kids" are, but I'd relate to them that the kids in Detroit were much kinder and more eager to engage with poetry. Detroit Public Schools students wholly embraced the opportunity to be given a voice. For many of my southern students it was difficult. Many would even apologize for what they wrote. It took viewings of movies like *Freedom Writers, Def Poetry Jam,* and *Mr. Holland's Opus,* the InsideOut video, CDs, and documentaries like *Louder than a Bomb* and *Slamnation.* It was always beautiful when the toughest, hardest, poorest, or most broken kid (north and south) would finally engage, slipping me the best poems—with instructions not to read aloud.

I remembered each child and how they were through their poetry. Matthew Severs was a Northwestern honor student, quiet, polite, and probably the most considerate, intriguing young man I have ever met. This excerpt is from his poem "Bullet Soul":

My soul is like a bullet,
Hot, active, strong, powerful,
Beautiful: willing to do what it can
To keep me alive, keep me new.

One day I will fly SO HIGH . . .
Across the FULL moon and I will juggle stars
I will soar into heaven and experience joy afar.

He wants to experience spaces, power, matter, and room. This is a metaphorical room or space for this poet. He is suggesting empowerment in space, even the literal cosmic space. He says his soul has grown so powerful it feels "like the boom of a nine mil" then states "better move off the spot," which is yet another space. The poet uses his soul as a metaphorical embodiment of his old neighborhood as he writes, "my body is an UZI, my soul is my shot, / a bullet soul is free / im a bullet but im not." In the poem "Curing the Incurables" he writes:

How does it feel, how does it feel, how does it lure,
living his life without a cure? Disease and demise drive
deeper and deeper the cries . . .
How does that teen trick stick on a creeper,
creeper, whose death is all knowing whose cells cure not,
where life is truly private, and crime is surely not? If sin had to
    begin
in this dim how did this teen row down deaths stream yo
swimming in slaughtered sorrows with no belief in tomorrow's?

He's a sad thought, seeking a cure while trying not to get caught in his meetings and greetings, through the "lick'ns, and stick'ns, / buck'n and kick'n, / testing then rest'n." In a poem about AIDS the poet advocates, "stay clean and cool / or do other choice actions like stay in school / wait on sex / or use protection / oppose the absurd / make your morals useful, make yourself heard." Then he speaks of dreaming and a bed in heaven. I later learned that Matthew and his mother were living in a homeless shelter at the time. It turned out to be one of the most painful moments I experienced because he was so deserving of a home of his own and I could not help him get there.

I was in the library one day when Alan Henderson stopped by my table. I was having a difficult day. Alan was a challenging student in school; he grimaced at my inquiries and was snarky, but he wrote well. He stopped to tell me he was writing poetry—and reading and reciting poetry at slams in Greensboro. I was shocked. He also said he was doing well in school and writing poetry was helping him. That is just one example of the many unexpected joys and paybacks that makes the struggle to teach poetry worthwhile.

When little kids (whose names I forget) run up, hug me and call me Mr. Poetry Man, or say *"That's the poetry man . . ."* if that connection to me has anything to do with enriching their critical thinking skills, helps close their achievement gaps, enhances their relationship to language, and makes them well-rounded, twenty-first-century students, I am obliged. Especially for the first through third graders whose reading scores mandate the number of prisons built in this country. To those kids I say thank you.

# Conclusion: Inside My Magic Pencil

*Peter Markus*

I hold up my pencil for everyone to see.

"Look at this pencil," I say.

I see thirty pairs of eyes giving this pencil of mine a look.

"It's not the handsomest pencil in this room," I point out. "I mean, there's nothing fancy about how this pencil looks. Right?

"On the surface," I say, "this pencil looks just like any other ordinary pencil."

I walk around the room, from student eye to student eye, so that everyone in this room has a chance to see what I want them to see.

Mr. Pete's magic pencil.

"Who wants to help Mr. Pete out?" I ask.

A flurry of hands raise up before I even say what I want help with.

"Look at this pencil," I say again. "What words would you use to describe this pencil?"

I hear words like dirty, beat-up, raggedy, rusty, stubby, burnt-looking, paint-chipped. The list goes on and on.

"It looks," one boy then says, his grin big and proud, "like it's been getting chewed on by a pitbull pup."

"Wow," I say. "Thank you. Boy oh boy, boys and girls, those are all good descriptive words to describe this pencil."

I tell them next to take a look at their own pencils, many of which have smiley faces or shimmery stars or yellowy pictures of Sponge-Bob SquarePants on them.

"Look at all these fancy-looking pencils," I say. "There are some really beautiful pencils with us in this room."

One girl, when she sees Mr. Pete's dirty, beat-up, raggedy, rusty, stubby, burnt-looking, paint-chipped pencil with no eraser on one end and a blunt tip of lead just barely sticking out from the front end of it, she offers me her shiny new pencil as a gift.

"Thanks," I say, "but no thanks. I've got the only pencil that I need."

My magic pencil.

I hold it up for all to see.

I give it a kiss.

"I've had this pencil for over thirty years," I tell them. "Since I was in the third grade," I say.

"That's a long time ago," someone says.

"It must be a magical pencil," someone else says.

"It is," I say. "But it's not like how a magic wand is magical," I want them to know. "I can't tap you twice on the top of your head and make you disappear into thin air."

I tap this one boy on top of the head. He does not disappear.

"And I can't turn you into a butterfly or a bird," I tell them, and a few of them, I can see, look up at me a bit disappointed.

I keep on telling them about all the things that I cannot do with my magic pencil.

"I can't fly," I say.

"I can't use it to make money grow on trees, or to pull a white rabbit out of a black hat."

I hold out my hands for them to see: they hold no money, no rabbit.

Only this grubby-looking pencil that looks like I've been digging in the dirt with it.

"I can't use it to dig down to China with," I say.

"What can it do, Mr. Pete?" is the question that one boy finally gets up the courage to ask.

"You want to know what my magic pencil can do?" I ask back.

Thirty heads bobble, up and down, yes, yes, yes.

I raise my pencil up to my eye.

I look inside.

I can see things with my magic pencil that nobody else in the world can see.

Anything that I want to see—if I want to see it badly enough, I can see it with my magic pencil.

"I can see my little son right now," I say.

I hold the pencil up to my eye, I tilt my head up, up towards the light.

"He's outside right now with his mama running around the house in his diaper," I say.

I keep watching my little boy running around inside the house.

I describe to them my son running, bare-footed, bare-chested, chasing after our dog.

"Uh-oh," I say, softly.

"Don't do that," I say, loud enough so that everyone can hear.

"That little stinker," I say, and I shake my head like I can't believe what I'm seeing.

"What's he doing?" the students are intrigued to know. "What did he do?"

"You don't want to know," I say.

"Tell us, Mr. Pete! Tell us!" I tell them that my little boy Solomon, who is two, just pulled off his diaper and took a pee in the middle of our house.

This gets some giggles and snickers and a few, "Ohh, that's nasty!"

"I've seen enough of that," I say. "I think I want to see something else."

So I take my pencil and I shake it like I'm shaking salt into a basket of French fries.

"I do this," I tell them. "I shake my pencil like this to keep the magic flowing so that I might see something new."

I raise the pencil back up to my eye.

I tell them that now, when I look inside my magic pencil, I see my granddad in his garden, raising up from his hands and knees, his thick white hair standing up, I say, like a dandelion gone to seed.

Then I tell them that my grandfather is dead, that he died a little over a month ago.

"But if he's dead, how can you see him?" someone asks.

"Good question," I say. "You want to know how?" I ask.

"How, Mr. Pete?"

"Because the people we love, " I say, and I nod my head, "live forever inside my magic pencil."

*   *   *

The next question is not *to be or not to be*. The question is *to see or not to see*.

"Who in this room," I say, "would like to have a magic pencil like Mr. Pete's?"

Sixty-odd eyes open wide.

Thirty-odd hands raise up the classroom roof.

"Good," I say. "Get ready."

I tell them to hold up their pencils to the light.

I tell them to hold onto them tight.

"What I'm gonna do," I say, "is I'm gonna go around the room, one by one, and I'm going to give you a little bit of Mr. Pete's magic.

"I'm going to tap your pencil twice," I tell them. "All it takes is two taps to get the magic going."

I tell them again to hold on tight. I tell them about the one time that I tapped this one little girl's pencil who wasn't holding on tight enough and the pencil flew out of her hand and out the window when I tapped some of Mr. Pete's magic into its tip.

I tell them about another time when another little boy wasn't holding onto his pencil tight enough and the pencil, with magic flowing through it, floated up out of this boy's hand and it got stuck, pencil-lead-first, into the ceiling of the room.

I see their tiny fingers clench into tiny knuckled fists around their waiting-to-be-turned-into-magic pencils.

I go around the room, one by one, student by student, and I tap each pencil twice.

"Get ready," I say.

"Hold on," I tell them again. "You ready?" I ask.

"Ready, Mr. Pete."

"Then let's let the magic begin."

The magic begins, I know—I believe—by getting the students to believe: to believe in the power and the magic of Mr. Pete's magic pencil.

"Hold up those magic pencils," I tell them. I say, "Repeat after me."

And here I begin the chant.

The incantation.
The prayer.
The song.
"I believe . . ."
*I believe.*
". . . in the power. . ."
*In the power.*
". . . of my magic pencil."
*Of my magic pencil.*
"When I look inside . . ."
*When I look inside.*
". . . my magic pencil . . ."
*My magic pencil.*
". . . I can see anything . . ."
*I can see anything.*
". . . that I want to see."
*That I want to see.*
"When I look inside . . ."
*When I look inside.*
". . . my magic pencil . . ."
*My magic pencil.*
". . . I can see anything . . ."
*I can see anything.*
". . . I can dream to see."
*I can dream to see.*
The song goes on.
"When I look inside . . ."
*When I look inside.*
". . . my magic pencil . . ."
*My magic pencil.*
". . . I can be . . ."
*I can be.*
". . . anything I want to be."
*Anything I want to be.*
"Because I believe . . ."
*Because I believe.*
". . . in the power . . ."

*In the power.*
". . . and the magic . . ."
*And the magic.*
". . . of my magic pencil."
*Of my magic pencil.*
"Inside my magic pencil . . ."
*Inside my magic pencil.*
". . . anything is possible."
*Anything is possible.*
"And the world . . ."
*And the world.*
". . . is mine . . ."
*Is mine.*
". . . to make."
*To make.*

Picture it: thirty-odd voices crying out these words, singing out these words, repeating what I want them to believe.

It's through the power of this incantation, through the mantra of these words, through the power of this prayer, that the world of this classroom is transformed into a holy place, a sacred chapel, and the students are miniature-sized angels in this make-believe, make-shift, magic pencil choir.

One magic pencil is powerful enough.

I tell the students this.

"But thirty magic pencils," I say, and I make my eyes as big as I can make them, "in the same room."

I shake my head as if this is too much power for one building to take, too much magic for one man to believe.

"The world as we know it," I warn them, and I can't help but grin. "The world will never be the same."

Transformed.

Transformation.

The change, I can see it in their faces, is beginning to take place.

On the count of one, two, three, I say.

\* \* \*

*Uno, dos, tres.*

It's time to take a look inside our magic pencils.

"On your mark," I say.

I tell them, "Get set."

I don't say go.

Not yet.

"Repeat after me," I say.

"I believe."

*I believe.*

"Believe in what?" I ask.

One boy answers, like the good listener that he is, "We believe in the power and the magic of our magic pencils."

"Give me some skin," I say, and I hold out my hand.

"But wait," I say. "I forgot to tell you something."

"What?"

I tell the students that I want them to be careful, that when they lift their magic pencils up to their eyes, I don't want them to stick or jab the pencil into their eyes. I don't want any eyeballs getting poked out and rolling around like marbles or hardboiled eggs across the classroom floor.

"This happened once before," I say.

I am not making this up.

"One time," I say, "at a school on the other side of the city, all of these little boy and little girl eyes were all rolling around the floor and Mr. Pete had to get down onto his hands and knees and pick all of those poked out eyeballs up and then I had to try to find which eyeballs fit into which eyeball sockets."

I let out a giant's sigh. I tell them it wasn't a pretty sight.

What is a pretty sight is seeing a classroom of thirty second graders with their pencils all raised in the air getting ready to look inside them.

Ready to look inside themselves.

We count to three. One, two, three. *Uno, dos, tres.* We lift our magic pencils up to our eyes.

"If you can dream it, you can see it," I say.

I ask, "What do you wish you could see?"

We are all of us in the midst of this seeing.

Some of the students are making sounds, oohs and ahhs, as if they are seeing fireworks on the Fourth of July.

Some of the students begin talking about what they see.

"We'll all have a chance to say what we saw," I say, "but for right now let's keep it to ourselves."

I tell them to keep looking.

"Thirty more seconds," I say.

Heads are craned upward, skyward, moonward, heavenward.

"The longer you look," I say, "the more you'll see."

We are all of us in this room looking for something that belongs to just us.

That is ours and ours alone to say.

I believe that this is true.

"Keep looking . . ."

"Ten more seconds . . ."

The countdown begins.

Ten, nine, eight, seven.

Six, five, four, three.

Two, I say. One.

Blastoff.

To be transported.

To come back down to this earth.

"Pencils down," I say.

No eyeballs have been lost.

These boys and girls are good listeners.

Now it's time to see if they are good seers.

"OK," I say. "That was beautiful."

I say, "Thank you."

I take a breath.

"So," I say. "Who saw something inside their magic pencil?"

Nearly all of the hands reach up toward the sky.

The heart beats a little faster.

The stars, I realize, are within our fingertips' reach.

"And who," I say next, "saw something they've never seen before?"

The hands that are raised up raise up even higher.

These fish, they've taken the make-believe bait.

They've swallowed the magic pencil hook.

Not even the constellations in the sky are safe.

The poet Jack Gilbert has a line in one of his poems that seems fitting for me to fit in at this point in this story.

*We must unlearn the constellations to see the stars.*

This line from Gilbert is fundamental to what I hope to do when I go into a classroom to teach.

To get the students to go, to look, to see beyond the surface of things.

To get these young seers, these visionaries, to go inside those places, those things: be it a pencil, a painting, a story, a stone—that are synonymous for that thing we call the self, the body, the heart.

This is just some of what these young seers see:

*I saw a man running down a dusty road until all that was left was dust.*

*I saw a robot with a triangle head and his eyes were like two boats and his body was like a TV and his hair was like light and his mouth was like a blue shoe and his legs were like a line and his feet were so big that one hundred people could fit under it.*

*I saw a river that looked like a chocolate river and the buildings looked like Snickers bars and the stars were made out of Laffy Taffy and the lights on the streets looked like ice cream cones and everybody ate everything up.*

*I saw a giant squid, it was purple, it had shiny teeth, it was eating a cheeseburger, it was writing a letter to Mr. Pete. It said, Dear Mr. Pete, I have a friend, his name is Bob. Your friend, Squid Joe.*

*I saw a tiger and a lion going to outer space. They had paper wings. The tiger didn't have a friend to play with so that's why the lion came and they became friends forever living in the same house.*

*I saw a huge eyeball. The eyeball was red. The white part of the eye was a rainbow.*

*I saw an elephant walking down the street, a dog talked to a boy with one leg, a dog in the sky with a book reading poems to the sun.*

*I saw a beautiful sunset and a rainbow too. We got some ice cream and then the sunset was gone. Then I saw stars and the moon with a face on it. And the moon was about to eat my ice cream cone and the man on the moon was about to eat me so I screamed and ran home in the dark.*

*I saw walking roses and an alien walking without breathing. I saw a flying stick up in the air, an eight-headed fish in a fishbowl walking on the sidewalk. I saw a shiny tooth jumping with a toothbrush and a man with one eye and a magic phone talking to a pony. Then I saw a girl named Lydia who looked a lot like me and whatever I did she did. And we were stuck together inside my pencil.*

*I saw a ninja in a black karate suit who was walking on top of a moving truck with a long stick in his hand that was brown. He was fighting bad guys. He punched someone so hard that he saw stars. Then he back-flipped off the truck and landed on his feet in an alley and took off his suit and went home to be with his family.*

*I saw an angel up in heaven. It was a woman in a blue dress. She had white wings and white teeth. She was smiling. Her hair was yellow. She was kind to kids. She was at a school. She was the teacher. She had a wand that was long. The wand was red and gray and striped. She liked to read to the kids. And she liked to draw pictures too. She was an artist. She had black eyebrows and long legs. Her legs were skinny. She was so tall she had to duck her head because the stars might hit her. She was beautiful.*

*I saw Africa's night sky. It was so beautiful I heard someone sing-
ing. I know love will find a way.*

I don't know what to say to this.

What is there to say to this?

Mr. Pete, Mr. Poet-Man, that man I am who always has something
to say, who always has a story to tell, is silenced by the good bounty
of these words. For me to speak, I think this to myself (though I do
not say it out loud), would almost be obscene.

To borrow again from poet Jack Gilbert, "I dream of lost vocabu-
laries that might express some of what we no longer can."

What I do say is this.

*Thank you. Thank you. Thank you.*

*Wow. Wow. Wow.*

But this is only the beginning.

"You saw," I say, "inside your pencil, a man running down a dusty
road until all that was left was dust?"

The boy whose eyes took him inside that place nods his head yes.

"You mean to tell me that there's a man inside your pencil?"

He smiles and nods his head again.

"Where was he running to?" I ask.

"He was running home to see his mama," he says.

"How come he was running and not walking?" I say.

"Because his father is dead."

I shake my head.

Here again, I don't know what to say when words like these rise
up, out of nowhere, and slap me in the face.

I am flabbergasted.

I am floored.

I want to lie down in some corner of this room and tuck my knees
in close to my face and weep for what this boy has just now said.

No, I want to run home to see my own father and throw my arms
around his neck.

I want to know more about that African night sky.

"Someone is singing," I say to the boy who saw this sky when he
looked inside his magic pencil.

Who is singing?

This is the question now.

I ask him who.

"Who is singing?" I say.

He says, "God is singing."

*God is singing.*

"Who is God singing to?" I ask.

"God is singing to the sky," he says.

"That's really beautiful," I say to this.

What else is there to say to this?

Sometimes silence, the sound of that sound, that momentary stillness, is the only sound that fits.

My brother John Rybicki, the most inspiring writing teacher I've ever seen teach, once wrote to me in a letter:

*When we sing, we are returning God back to God.*

Here, at this point in this story, I think Rybicki's words fit.

But it's also true that not everyone has heard the sound of God singing. And it's true too that not everyone in this room who has a magic pencil in his or her hand sees something when they lift it up to their eye and look inside it.

A handful of students did not raise up their hands when I asked them the question, "Who saw something inside their magic pencil?"

Which is OK.

Which is expected.

Sometimes you have to look twice.

I tell them all, even those who saw something the first time they looked, to take up their pencils.

"Get ready. Get set. On the count of one, two, three," I say. "Uno, dos, tres."

I count us down.

Work down, build up.

"Now shake," I say, and I show them how to shake it good.

"Your pencil is no longer a pencil," I tell them. "Your pencil is now a salt shaker. Shake it up," I say. "This'll get the magic flowing."

Thirty-odd fists are shaking salt over baskets of imaginary French fries. There is so much salt flying around in this classroom it's as if we are trapped inside a snow globe with snow falling from the sky.

A few months from now, when it is full-on winter here in Detroit, I will ask the students to look inside a snowflake.

"No two snowflakes," I will tell them, "are exactly alike."

What they see, when they look inside, is further proof of this.

I will also ask them questions like, *What does snow falling from the sky sound like if you listen real close? What does snow falling from the sky look like if you look real close?*

In short, I am inviting them to pay attention to the world around them: to see what others fail to see.

But back to those magic pencils.

So we're shaking them hard.

Salt, or snow, depending on how you want to look at it, is making a whiteout blizzard of the classroom.

The magic inside those magic pencils is flowing.

It is flowering.

"OK," I say. "Time to take a look."

But first. We need to say again the Pledge of the Magic Pencil.

"I believe . . ."

*I believe.*

". . . in the power . . ."

*In the power.*

". . . and the magic . . ."

*And the magic.*

". . . of my magic pencil."

*Of my magic pencil.*

"When I look inside . . ."

*When I look inside.*

". . . my magic pencil . . ."

*My magic pencil.*

". . . anything . . ."

*Anything.*

". . . no everything . . ."

*No everything.*

"Is possible."

*Is possible.*

You get the picture.

Words are taking us to that place.

Words, these words, chanted like this, pledged like this, are opening that door.

Call it the trapdoor to the eternal.

The sublime.

And so we lift up those magic pencils up to our eyes. We open that door.

We look inside.

The question next is this:

"Who saw something this time when you looked inside your magic pencil?"

Here again, most of the hands raise up as if to fingertip-touch the ceiling tiles, including a couple of kids whose hands had not raised up the first time I asked that question—students, in other words, whose eyes had not seen anything when they looked the first time inside their magic pencils.

I am, of course, pleased by what I see.

This is some of what the students saw the second time they looked inside:

*I saw a nine-headed skeleton and a dragon fighting each other.*

*I saw a goldfish with a dark purple hat walking down the street.*

*I saw a monster with one eye and three legs. He was bigger than me. He could walk all the way from Michigan to China. He was bigger than fifty school buses. He was bigger than a big cruise boat. He was bigger than heaven.*

*I saw a monster chained up. His eyes were round and inside they were yellow and red. He had little cursive pictures on his feet. He was as big as two buildings put together. He attacked with fireballs coming out of his hands. His chains were swinging. He was knocking down houses. He knocked down the Empire State Building. He stepped on trees. He drank all the water to get more power. He destroyed every school in the world.*

*I saw a monster with red eyes. He was as big as this building is. He was so big if he took one step he could cross the Detroit River. He had silver wings that were made out of metal. He blew fire from his mouth. He blew fire at the Empire State Building but no one got hurt. He could jump up to heaven. He could pick up a planet in one hand. He ate the Twin Towers and then he ate the Statue of Liberty. Then he flew to Mars and set it on fire. Then he ate the sun and he was still hungry so he ate a meteor. Then he ate every planet in the world.*

*I saw two men with six eyes and one foot. They had red and blue hats on and their noses were orange. Their names were Poch and Boch. They had black and red shoes on and they both had a red face. I saw a strange dog with them too. The color of the dog was red too. And I saw a monster too. He had red and blue eyes. He was scary. He was so scary that I felt like I was about to fall out of a car.*

*I saw a monster that blew fire at this building. He made a noise that hurt my ears. So I got a jar and put him in there but then he got out and destroyed the rest of the city.*

As you can see, seeing monsters became a bit contagious.

But words and pictures inspire like words and pictures.

It's the power of language to shape the world and the way in which we see it.

I can't help but believe that things are looking up.

Hafiz, the great Sufi poet from the fourteenth century, once wrote that, "Our words become the house we live in."

I can't help but picture now a house made of words.

It is a beautiful house.

# Contributors

ALISE ALOUSI's poems have appeared in *Graffiti Rag*, *The Alternative Press*, *The Malpais Review*, and in several anthologies including *We Are Iraqis: Aesthetics and Politics in a Time of War* (Syracuse University Press). She is a Knight Arts Challenge recipient for *From Detroit to Baghdad: Al-Mutanabbi Street Starts Here*.

TERRY BLACKHAWK, a former high school creative writing teacher, founded InsideOut Literary Arts Project in 1995 in order to bring the power of poetry and literary self-expression to youth in Detroit classrooms. She is the author of four full-length collections of poetry including *Escape Artist* (BkMk Press), winner of the 2003 John Ciardi Prize, and *The Light Between* (Wayne State University Press, 2012). She was twice named Michigan Creative Writing Teacher of the Year through the Michigan Youth Arts Festival and received the 2010 Pablo Neruda Poetry Prize from *Nimrod International* and the Michigan Governor's Award for Arts Education. Blackhawk holds an honorary doctorate as well as a PhD from Oakland University and is a 2013 Kresge Arts in Detroit Literary Fellow.

NORENE CASHEN is a writer-in-residence with InsideOut Literary Arts Project in Detroit. For two years she served as the coordinator for Citywide Poets, Detroit's youth poetry slam team. Her poems have been published in *Exquisite Corpse*, markszine.com, *Adanna Literary Journal*, *Temenos*, *Quill Puddle*, *Detroit: Stories* (MOCAD), *Dispatch Detroit*, and the anthology *Abandon Automobile* (Wayne State University Press, 2001). Her first collection of poems, *The Reverse Is Also True*, was published by Doorjamb Press in 2007 and re-released as a Dzanc rEprint Series Ebook in 2013. She's a former freelance arts journalist. Her articles and reviews have appeared in *Metro Times* (Detroit), *Your Flesh Quarterly*, *Orbit*, *The Orlando Weekly*, *New Times* (Kansas City), *The Rocket*, *ROCKRGRL Magazine*, and other publications.

ANNA CLARK is an independent journalist living in Detroit. She has written for *The New Republic*, NBC News online, *Pacific Stan-*

*dard, The American Prospect, Salon,* and other publications. She's a former Fulbright fellow in Kenya, where she focused on creative writing. In 2012, she founded Literary Detroit. Her writing was a "notable" pick in *Best American Sports Writing 2012* and she is a political media correspondent for the *Columbia Journalism Review*. She is also a founding board member of Write a House and a contributing editor for *Waxwing Literary Journal*. Anna edited *A Detroit Anthology*, a collection of essays, poetry, photography, and art that was published in 2014. She graduated from the University of Michigan and from Warren Wilson College's MFA Program for Writers.

NANDI COMER received a joint MFA/MA in Poetry and African American and African Diaspora Studies at Indiana University. She has received fellowships from Virginia Center for the Arts, Cave Canem, and Callaloo. Her poems have appeared or are forthcoming in *A Detroit Anthology* (Rust Belt Chic Press, 2014), in *Another and Another: An Anthology From the Grind Daily Writing Series* (Bull City Press, 2012), *Cave Canem Anthology XII* (Willow Books 2012),*Callaloo, Crab Orchard Review, Spoon River Poetry Review, Sycamore Review,* and *Third Coast.*

ROBERT FANNING is the author of *American Prophet* (Marick Press), *The Seed Thieves* (Marick Press), and *Old Bright Wheel* (Ledge Press Poetry Award). His poems have appeared in *Poetry, Ploughshares, Shenandoah, The Atlanta Review,* and other journals. A graduate of the University of Michigan and Sarah Lawrence College, he is Associate Professor of Creative Writing at Central Michigan University. He is also the founder and facilitator of the Wellspring Literary Series in Mt. Pleasant, Michigan, where he lives with his wife, sculptor Denise Whitebread Fanning, and their two children. To read more of his work, visit www.robertfanning.wordpress.com.

ARICKA FOREMAN's work has appeared or is forthcoming in *The Drunken Boat, Torch Poetry: A Journal for African American Women, Minnesota Review, Union Station Magazine, Vinyl Poetry,* and the YA anthology *Please Excuse This Poem: 100 New Poems for the Next Generation* by Viking Penguin (April 2015). She is currently an MFA candidate in Poetry at Cornell University, and has received fellowships from Cave Canem and the Callaloo Writers Workshop. She is a poetry editor for *Muzzle Magazine*.

CINDY FRENKEL's poetry and prose has been featured in such diverse publications as *The MacGuffin*, *Renaissance City*, *Vanity Fair*, and *The New York Observer*, where she was a columnist. She wrote and edited the Detroit Institute of Arts magazine and co-authored 100 *Essential Books for Jewish Readers*. Frenkel earned her MFA from Columbia University while working on *The New Yorker*'s editorial staff. She began her affiliation with InsideOut Literary Arts Project in 2009 as a writer-in-residence. She also tutors, edits, and teaches creative writing to adults; additionally, she is an adjunct professor at Oakland Community College, Lawrence Technological University, Wayne State University, and the Art Institute of Michigan.

FRANCINE J. HARRIS's first collection, *allegiance* (Wayne State University Press, 2012), was a finalist for the 2013 Kate Tufts Discovery and PEN Open Book Award. Her work has appeared, or is forthcoming, in *Poetry, Boston Review, Rattle, Ninth Letter,* and *Ploughshares* among others. Originally from Detroit, she is a Cave Canem fellow and a member of the creative writing faculty at Interlochen Center for the Arts.

STACY PARKER LE MELLE is the author of *Government Girl: Young and Female in the White House* (Ecco/HarperCollins). She is the workshop director for the Afghan Women's Writing Project and chronicles stories for *The Katrina Experience*, an Oral History Project. She also served as primary contributor to *McSweeney's Voices from the Storm: The People of New Orleans on Hurricane Katrina and Its Aftermath*. Her essays have appeared in *Apogee Journal* and on Salon.com. She blogs on politics and the arts for *The Huffington Post*. She is the founder of Harlem Against Violence & Homophobia and is the co-founder of the First Person Plural Reading Series. More information is available at www.stacyparkeraab.com.

PETER MARKUS is the Senior Writer with the InsideOut Literary Arts Project and has been a writer-in-residence with iO since its inception. He is the author of the novel *Bob, or Man on Boat,* as well as five other books of short fiction, the most recent of which is *The Fish and the Not Fish*. His fiction has appeared widely in such journals as the *Iowa Review, Chicago Review, Black Warrior Review, Quarterly West, Denver Quarterly, Massachusetts Review*, among many others. He was a Kresge Arts in Detroit fellow in Literary Arts in 2012.

JAMAAL MAY is the author of *Hum* (Alice James Books), which received the American Library Association's Notable Book Award, *Foreword Review*'s IndieFab Silver Medal, an NAACP Image Award nomination, and was named one of *The Boston Globe*'s Best Books of 2013. His poetry has received over a dozen awards, including a Spirit of Detroit Award, Pushcart Prize, and a Civitella Ranieri Fellowship in Italy. Recent work appears from NYTimes.com, *Poetry, The New Republic, The Believer, Ploughshares*, and *Best American Poetry 2014*. Jamaal is a Kenyon Review Fellow and co-directs Organic Weapon Arts with Tarfia Faizullah.

ISAAC MILLER is an MFA candidate in Poetry at New York University. He has taught with InsideOut Literary Arts Project, Detroit Future Schools, the James and Grace Lee Boggs School, and Youth Speaks. Originally from California, Isaac graduated from UC Berkeley with degrees in Ethnic Studies and Interdisciplinary Studies and received the Judith Lee Stronach Baccalaureate Prize. His writing has appeared or is forthcoming in *The Collagist, Muzzle Magazine, Midwestern Gothic, Watershed Review, English Journal*, and the anthology *Uncommon Core: Contemporary Poems for Learning and Living*.

CHACE "MIC WRITE" MORRIS, a slam poet, is the 2010 Detroit Grand Slam Champion and the 2010 Rustbelt Individual Slam Champion, and is a former member of four Detroit National Slam Teams. Morris was featured in the *Metro Times* list of "Top 5 Poets in Detroit" and has opened for acts such as Talib Kweli, The Last Poets, and RZA of the Wu Tang Clan. Morris is a member of the acclaimed hip-hop collective Cold Men Young. He received a Kresge Arts in Detroit Fellowship in Literary Arts in 2013.

GLORIA NIXON-JOHN has a BS and MA from Wayne State University and a PhD from Michigan State University. She has published essays, fiction, and poetry in small, mainstream, and online presses. Three of her poems have recently appeared in *Clover*, a publication of the Independent Writers' Studio in Bellingham,

Washington. Gloria has also published pedagogical chapters and articles in many books and journals. Her novel, *The Killing Jar*, based on the story of one of the youngest Americans to serve on death row, was published in 2012. Her memoir, *Learning from Lady Chatterley*, will be published in 2015.

MATTHEW OLZMANN's first book of poems, *Mezzanines*, received the 2011 Kundiman Prize and was published by Alice James Books. His writing has appeared or is forthcoming in *Brevity*, *New England Review*, *The Kenyon Review*, *Poetry Northwest*, *The Southern Review*, and elsewhere. Currently, he is a Visiting Professor of Creative Writing in the undergraduate writing program at Warren Wilson College.

KRISTIN PALM is a Detroiter now living in Oakland, California, where she works in community development and continues to teach poetry in the schools. She worked for InsideOut from 1999 to 2002, teaching at several Detroit high schools, leading City-wide Poets, and coaching the organization's first slam team. Her first book, *The Straits*, was published in 2008 by the serendipitously named Palm Press. Her writing has also appeared in the anthologies *Bay Poetics* (Faux Press, 2006) and *Abandon Automobile* (Wayne State University Press, 2001), and numerous journals, magazines, and newspapers, including *Metropolis*, *Crain's Detroit Business*, and the *Detroit Metro Times*.

THOMAS PARK lives and teaches in Warrenton, North Carolina, where he is developing the Warren Artists' Market (WAM), a writers' collective and after-school literary arts program. He received his MFA from Goddard College and MA in English from Wayne State University. He has been published in *The Wayne Review*, *structural arc*, *West Trade Review*, *Best New Poets*, and *The Pitkin Review*.

JULIA PUTNAM is a proud to have been born and raised in Detroit. She studied English Literature at Michigan State University and studied for her teaching certificate while serving as a writer-in-residence at InsideOut. At InsideOut, she also coordinated the Tell Your Family Story program for parents at Central High School and had the honor of working with Naomi Long Madgett. Currently, she is a co-founder and the principal of the community-based James and Grace Lee Boggs School on the east side of Detroit. Its mission is to nurture creative, critical thinkers who contribute to the well-being of their communities.

JOHN RYBICKI is the author of three collections of poetry, *Traveling at High Speeds* (New Issues Press), *We Bed Down into Water* (Triquarterly Books), and *When All the World Is Old* (LookOut Books). His poems have appeared widely in such publications as *Poetry*, *Paris Review*, *Ploughshares*, *North American Review*, as well as in both the 2008 and 2009 editions of *The Best American Poetry*.

SUZANNE SCARFONE, widely published poet, English Romantic Poetry and Virginia Woolf scholar, is a writer-in-residence with InsideOut Literary Arts Project in Detroit; a creative writing professor and curriculum advisor with the Afghan Women's Writing Project; a hospital healing arts poetry consultant; and a university lecturer. She has produced two music and poetry compact discs, The Poetry Harmonium and Arts at an Exhibition, and has received two poetry awards from the Wayne County Council for Arts, History, and Humanities. She has most recently co-authored *Lessons from Afghanistan: A Curriculum for Exploring Themes of Love and Forgiveness*, a collaborative project of the Afghan Women's Writing Project and the Fetzer Institute. She was educated at Michigan State University and Wayne State University, where she earned her PhD in English Literature with cognates in Art History, French Literature, and Old English. Empathy for the vulnerable child, the aged sick, the weary wanderer, and the soul on the brink of change underlies all of her poetry.

ANITA SCHMALTZ—painter, writer, photographer, and singer-songwriter—earned a BFA from College for Creative Studies for painting and a Masters of Creative Writing from Wayne State University in Detroit, the city where she was born. She's written reviews and articles on performing arts for the *Metro Times*, and teaches creative writing in Detroit public schools through the InsideOut Literary Arts Project. Schmaltz lives in Metro Detroit where she teaches creativity workshops, writes, paints, and performs in her music project TeleVision Faerie Tale (TVFT). More information is available at www.anitaschmaltz.com

KRISTINE UYEDA is a Kundiman fellow whose poems and microfiction have appeared in the journals *Rattle, Cyphers, Lantern Review, The Collagist*, and *Boxcar Poetry Review*. Kristine has been the recipient of numerous awards and scholarships, most recently a Penland School of Crafts Winter Residency and a Walker Scholarship from the Provincetown Fine Arts Work Center. She holds an MFA in Creative Writing/Poetry from Vermont College of Fine Arts.